Stranger in the Wings

GS Misc 532

Stranger in the Wings

Advisory Board of Ministry

Policy Paper No. 8

CHURCH HOUSE PUBLISHING

Church House Publishing
Church House
Great Smith Street
London
SW1P 3NZ

ISBN 07151 2601 6

Published 1998 for the Advisory Board of Ministry of the General Synod
by Church House Publishing

Second impression 1999

Cover design by Peggy Chapman
Printed in England by The Cromwell Press Ltd, Trowbridge, Wiltshire

Contents

Members of the Working Party

Chairman: The Rt Revd Bill Ind, Bishop of
                             Grantham (Bishop of Truro from
                             September 1997)

Members: Mrs Margaret Baxter, Member of the
                             Advisory Board of Ministry until 1997;
                             Assistant to Diocesan Director of
                             training; Director of Reader Training for
                             Blackburn; Member of General Synod,
                             and a Reader since 1971.

                             Canon Andrew Bowden,
                             Rector of Coates, diocese of Gloucester;
                             Author of Ministry in the Countryside.

                             The Revd Wendy Bracegirdle,
                             Principal of Manchester LNSM Scheme.

Secretary: The Revd Roy Screech,
                             Selection Secretary and LNSM
                             Co-ordinator (Senior Selection
                             Secretary from January 1997).

The Working Party is grateful to Dr Caroline Mills, Principal Lecturer in Geography at the Cheltenham and Gloucester College of Higher Education, for her work on the survey of LNSMs, and to the Revd David Leslie, Team Rector of Ditton in the Diocese of Liverpool, for Appendix 5 on Transformative Education.

Preface

During the last four years there has been a rapid increase in the number of dioceses which have submitted Local Non-Stipendiary Ministry schemes for approval by the House of Bishops. There are now sixteen such schemes, which have built on the pioneering work undertaken in Lincoln, Truro, Manchester and Southwark.

A new Working Party report is therefore timely in reviewing current developments in Local Ministry and offering a theological and sociological rationale for this new form of ordained ministry. The 28 recommendations contained in the report build on those which were made in the first report on LNSM (ABM Policy Paper No. 1, April 1991). The House of Bishops debated *Stranger in the Wings* in January 1998, and endorsed the recommendations.

I am pleased to commend *Stranger in the Wings* to a wide audience. It traces the history of the emergence of Local Non-Stipendiary Ministry, describes some of the difficulties which have been encountered and the ways in which they have been overcome, and draws attention to the remarkable way in which new vocations to ordination have been fostered, and the Church's whole ministry has been extended and enriched. LNSM is by no means the only important development in ministry, but I believe it is one which needs to be more widely known and understood, and I am confident that this report will be a very significant contribution to the debate about how the Church's whole ministry can be more effective in the service of the gospel and the kingdom.

✠ John Hereford
Chairman
Advisory Board of Ministry

Acknowledgements

The publisher gratefully acknowledges permission to reproduce copyright material in this book. Every effort has been made to trace and contact copyright holders. If there are any inadvertent omissions we apologize to those concerned and will ensure that a suitable acknowledgement is made at the next reprint.

CareerTrack, Inc.: Diagram from *Workbook: How to Lead a Team*, 1996 (p. 48).

David Higham Associates: Extract from Louise Macneice, 'Mutations', from *Collected Poems*, Faber & Faber (p. 1).

Prentice-Hall, Inc., Upper Saddle River, NJ: Diagram from David A. Kolb, *Experiential Learning: Experience as the Source of Learning and Development*, © 1984. Reprinted by permission (p. 123).

CHAPTER 1

The stranger in the wings

For every static world that you or I impose
Upon the real one must crack at times and new
Patterns from new disorders open like a rose
And old assumptions yield to new sensation;
The stranger in the wings is waiting for his cue,
The fuse is always laid to some annunciation.

Louis MacNeice, 'Mutations'

1.1   It is six years since an Advisory Board of Ministry Working Party
produced ABM Policy Paper No. 1 called 'Local NSM'. That Working
Party covered at least some of the same ground as the present Working
Party and it may be wondered therefore why there is a need so quickly for
another report. 'Local NSM' looked at all the major issues and made
important recommendations. These recommendations have broadly
become policy since 1991. The recommendations made in the current
report build on the theological work done and recommendations made in
the 1991 document. Moreover, throughout the nineties there have been
discussions in many dioceses about LNSM. These discussions have been
both formal and informal, in synods and chapters, in deaneries and
parishes. Also in 1994, the Edward King Institute organized an international consultation about local ministry and has plans for another in 1998.

1.2   So, in the last six years, local ministry in its different forms and
manifestations has received a great deal of attention, both from people
directly concerned with its theology and practice and also from people in
parishes and settings which differ widely from each other. Perhaps this

interest in itself justifies another report but there are other very important reasons for this work, commissioned by ABM.

1.3   First of all there is now a significant number of ordained local ministers working in different dioceses in England, and interesting proposals are being made in the diocese for Europe. The Working Party commissioned a survey with a questionnaire professionally designed and evaluated. This was sent to all known ordained local ministers, eighty-three in all, and sixty-five replies were received. The questionnaire was detailed and thorough and gives invaluable information about LNSM. The outline questionnaire is included as Appendix 3 to this report and various quotations and statistics are included within the main body of the text.

1.4   In this introduction it is important to refer to the first key point mentioned by Dr Caroline Mills who designed and evaluated the survey. 'First, respondents overwhelmingly reported LNSM as a very positive experience, bringing them great joy and happiness, the role of the LNSM as a community priest with special knowledge was viewed as a productive ministry.'

1.5   Secondly, there have been important, not to say dramatic changes in the Church of England since 1991. The effect of the problems of the Church Commissioners has been very great, not just in financial or structural terms, but in more subtle ways. There has been a shift from seeing the Commissioners as a provider of money and resources and, above all perhaps, of security. There is a feeling in dioceses that they are more on their own than ever before.

1.6   Of course each diocese has always had its own identity, life and style, indeed the Church of England has been described often as forty-four separate corner shops. To continue though with that image, it is as if now, the wholesaler, with whom all the shops have been dealing, is perceived to be in trouble and may be even going bankrupt and the shopkeepers are wondering exactly what the future holds for them.

1.7   Everyone knows that an enormous amount of work has been done and that great structural changes have been made, but even if they are successful there has still been a shift in perception and attitudes. There are real questions around about whether there is enough money for the Church to survive in its present institutional form.

1.8   Alongside this, related to it but also separate from it, there was the significant drop in the numbers of men and women offering themselves for stipendiary ministry. The issues surrounding this are covered in the ABM Working Party report of 1996 called *Recovering Confidence* and there is no need to rehearse the various statistics and arguments found there, but they are relevant as part of the background to the thinking of this report.

1.9   All of this has affected the Church in many different ways and not least among those, it has affected those responsible for the provision of traditional theological education. For example in the College of the Resurrection Mirfield Newsletter of 1996, there are a couple of sentences which illustrate this change. 'The number of NSM candidates in training will very soon match that of stipendiary candidates in training, about 525 of each. The greatest growth is that of local non-stipendiary ministry related to Diocesan Schemes.'

1.10   These facts are important because, as dioceses have been planning their strategies for ministry, they have been aware that there is uncertainty about money in the short to medium term, and also a shortage of men and women offering themselves for stipendiary ministry.

1.11   At the same time, there is evidently in many dioceses, especially those that are predominantly rural, a desire to keep church buildings open and in use regularly, if not weekly, for worship. Obviously there are exceptions to this but there is much local support for this policy and the common experience is that money is found more easily to pay for the repair and maintenance of church buildings than for the support of the ministry that goes on in and around those buildings.

1.12   There is determination too in the urban areas, to maintain an active Christian presence in the inner cities and the outer housing estates and once again this has the broad support, not just of committed Christians, but of men and women of goodwill who value the presence and the resources which the Church provides. And they know, from their own experience, that the local church can have a much more local feel and shape than any other 'national' institution. It is a potent source of hope.

1.13   In order to meet both needs and expectations, there has to be a strategy which does not rely as heavily and completely on stipendiary clergy. It is therefore not an accident that it was a very large, mainly rural diocese, Lincoln, and a large urban diocese with great problems in the inner city and outer housing estates, Manchester, which began in a coherent way to explore and develop a policy of local ministry. These two dioceses, in their very different ways, felt the pressure and responded to it strategically before anyone else. They were conscious in so doing that they were breaking the mould. It was not for them a last ditch attempt to plug gaps but, on the contrary, an attempt to put in place a strategy for the changed situation. (This is not to say that there weren't people who had been thinking about this kind of strategy before. The writing for instance of Canon John Tiller, when he was Chief Secretary of ACCM, and also the work done by the Revd Ted Roberts at Bethnal Green described in his book, *Partners and Ministers*, have been important in helping to shape later thinking.)

1.14   At the same time it remains true that there are many bishops and dioceses who have not been convinced by the arguments in favour of Local Non-Stipendiary Ministry. There are some perhaps who believe that there has not been enough theological discussion, so inevitably there has been debate and criticism. All sorts of questions have been raised. What does local mean? What does collaboration mean? What are the functions respectively of the priests and lay people? How can we define relationships and the role of the wider Church and of the bishop in Local Ministry? What form should training take for this form of ministry? Should the LNSM candidates and those training for more traditional forms of ministry train together? What happens when a new appointment is made in a parish? What is the difference between Readers and local ministers? Why don't we simply ordain Readers? In answer to the last question, Readers will often be members of a Local Ministry Team. Some will be called by the community to minister as priests, and will gladly accept that calling. In that case they will also accept the need for a training which allows them to grow into that priestly calling. Other Readers feel themselves called to a ministry of preaching and teaching, but know that their distinctive ministry is to be lay. The other questions we respond to elsewhere in the text.

1.15   These are just some of the questions that have been raised and the arrival of Local Ministry has meant that these questions and many more, have been brought to the fore. It is important to see that these are not new questions, though they are perhaps focused in a new way. Local Ministry, like Ecumenism, is making the Church face these questions, not just in an academic theological way, but in a way that affects directly ordinary, everyday, Christian living.

1.16   They are questions that cannot be ignored because now more than one-third of the dioceses of the Church of England have had Local Ministry schemes approved by the House of Bishops and there are more in the pipeline. Some dioceses have debated the questions and have decided this is not a path that they wish to go down. However, even they have had to ask themselves the question, 'If not Local Ministry in one form or another, then what?'

1.17   In many places the traditional pattern of ministry is under strain, and some would say that in a few places it has actually broken down. This has meant there has been a search for different ways of providing ministry. In some dioceses, for instance, there has been the provision of a house for duty for a recently retired priest, in others an emphasis on recruiting NSMs or ordaining Readers. And it is in this context and against this background that Local Non-Stipendiary Ministry has developed. It is part of a changing pattern of ordained ministry. In some dioceses it has been seen as just one relatively small element in a ministerial strategy, while in others it has become more central and significant.

1.18   The changing pattern is highlighted in the editorial of *Theology* in January/February 1998:

> In 1966, 470 candidates were recommended for training for ordination . . . In 1996, 178 men were recommended for training for ordination to stipendiary ministry as priests in the Church of England, but that is not the whole story for that Church. In 1996, 66 women were recommended for training for stipendiary ministry as priests and 63 men and 72 women were recommended for training for non-stipendiary ministry, and 42 men and 30 women were recommended to train for Local Non-Stipendiary Ministry as priests, giving a total of 451 people recommended for training for ordination to priestly ministry in the Church of England in 1996 compared with 470 in 1966.

1.19   Community is a key concept in Christian thinking, but it is itself open to all sorts of questions. Andrew Marr in *Ruling Britannia* says, 'Community has become the intellectually responsible form of nostalgia but also the propaganda of optimists everywhere' (p. 321). But he goes on a few pages later to say, 'Yet it would be wrong to brush aside this contemporary fascination with community as illiberal or irrelevant. It may be vague, even woolly. It may not be a new idea. It may be open to abuse. But it is also quite simply a return to the values that have sustained human society for a very long time and which seem pertinent today precisely because of the opposite pressures of globalisation.'

1.20   This is part of the context in which we need to see our thinking about Local Ministry and the sustaining of local church life. It is something we do representatively as part of society and in our own way on behalf of society. As John Tinsley, Bishop of Bristol, said in an address to the Bristol Diocesan Synod in November 1976, 'To sum up, the Church of England must never be more interested in herself than she is in England. Her mission is to think about England in the light of the Christian Faith.'

1.21   As we have visited local schemes, written to different people, had conversations, the members of the Working Party have been impressed by the enthusiasm and commitment of those who are trying to work out the implications of their faith in this very new situation. We believe they need our support and our understanding. That is not to say that everything they are doing should be uncritically commended, but they are, without a doubt, people who are taking seriously the place of the Church in the lives of local people.

CHAPTER 2

What is local?

2.1   This century has seen a remarkable theological re-valuing of the local congregation within Anglicanism; and LNSM is part of this process. But should we be putting so many eggs in the 'local' basket? It is perhaps worth taking a step sideways and looking at 'local' through the eyes of geographers and anthropologists.

Physical space

2.2   We inherit a concept of local which is largely geographical. 'The local' means 'the alehouse around the corner'. A 'local' boy is one who comes from 'our' town or village. The parish is defined by rigid geographical divisions marked on the landscape (the bounds), and more recently on the map.

2.3   Technology has of course 'exploded' this concept of local. The wheel, printing, the bicycle, the car, radio and television, the aeroplane and cyberspace mean that today the only truly 'local' places left on the planet are perhaps in the jungles of New Guinea. Indeed, for most working people (and for many at school), there is now a clear geographical distinction between where they work and where they live.

2.4   We can see the change if we consider the variety of meanings we now give to the word local. 'Local' government is organized at county rather than parish level. We refer to a 'local' accent meaning the brogue often heard in a 'locality' rather than in a particular place (Professor Higgins notwithstanding!); and 'local' landscape characteristics are often thought of as common to a 'region'. It could indeed be argued that the 'Region' – the Highlands, the Borders, the Lakes – is as important a locus for what we today generally mean by 'local' as the individual settlement.

2.5   We live then in a world which has long outgrown the parish boundary — a 'multi-boundaried' society in which 'local' changes from minute to minute, depending on who we are talking to.

Social space

2.6   Closely related to the concept of 'local' is that slippery concept of 'community'. (A recent paper sets out no fewer than 96 different uses of the term in academic journals!) The pioneering social studies of traditional British villages — (such as Williams, *The Sociology of an English Village: Gosforth*) — suggested that villages have always consisted of an assemblage of discrete but interlocking 'communities', dependent on blood relationship, employment, wealth, not to mention neighbourhood within the village.

2.7   Indeed, one of the key problems of many local churches is that the communities which built them have changed their nature. In most villages the parish church building is still a 'focus' of community for most of the 'communities' within the settlement. But even in a village the congregation who worship in that parish church are often perceived as a 'club' — or by themselves as one 'community' among all the others.

2.8   Later social studies quoted in the chapter on 'community' in *The People, the Land and the Church* (Diocese of Hereford,1987, pp. 26ff.), show how in a modern village every household 'networks' with a variety of communities which do not necessarily overlap, and many of which stretch far beyond the village. Seeking to analyse this, geographers have drawn a distinction between 'physical space' and 'social space'. 'Social space' is the physical space in which an individual actually operates. They point out that different individuals who share the same physical space often live their lives quite differently. The 'social space' of a boy who belongs to Scouts, is keen on amateur dramatics, and plays in a football team, will be different from the social space of his sister who goes to the same school, but whose friends live in the village; and from his grandmother who, though she lives with the family, is housebound.

2.9   To those living outside the 'physical space' of the settlement it may be convenient to regard those who live there as one 'local community'. But those who live within that physical space are likely to experience it rather as, what Anthony Russell called, 'a battleground for competing interest groups'. And although that physical space is special for each of them, it is for each of them merely the base from which they sally forth to a variety of 'wide-ranging activities in far-flung lands'.

Image and reality

2.10   A third factor which is re-moulding our idea of 'local' is the media. We are bombarded with images, so that the dividing line between reality and image begins to waver. Disneyland seeks to make us experience the image as 'real' – and so do television travel documentaries. Increasingly we find ourselves believing that the 'real' Cotswolds are the carefully manicured streams and verges of Upper and Lower Slaughter (which probably last saw a sheep in 1939), rather than the housing estates on the edge of Stow-on-the-Wold where people really live. Similarly we accept as a 'real' farm the Guiting Power Farm Park with its collection of rare breeds and its pets corner; rather than Guiting Manor Farm over the road with its rack of grain silos and its modern tractor sheds.

2.11   Of course artists have always influenced our perception of beauty. Michael Mayne in *This Sunrise of Wonder* illustrates how W. M. Turner changed the way we see landscape by a nice quotation from Oscar Wilde's 'The Decay of Lying'.

> Yesterday evening Mrs Arundel insisted on my going to the window and looking at the glorious sky, as she called it. Of course I had to look at it . . . and what was it? It was simply a very second-rate Turner, a Turner of a bad period, with all the painter's worst faults exaggerated and over-emphasised.

But the great artists help us to see better what is 'really' there. By contrast, the image makers of today are all too often working in the tradition of those sentimentalists who wanted to shield the sensitive eyes of their upper-class patrons from the reality of life around them.

2.12   'Local' is often used today to promote a particular culture. (This is especially true of rural life where imagined 'honest simplicity' has always been the literary foil of urban 'wickedness'.) In a recent article, Cloke and Milbourne argue that people use 'local', not only to keep themselves sane, but also to underpin certain conservative ethical standards. 'The culture of country life has been sanitised in today's countryside and through the ideology of idyll, the countryside is involved with meanings associated with patriotism, conservation, patriarchy, ethnic and class relations.' Where 'local' becomes escapist costume drama there is a clear danger of idolatry.

2.13   All of these points might suggest that the Church is being foolish, if not positively devious in concentrating on 'local' – were it not that, for most people most of the time, 'local' is still very important indeed.

THE CONTINUING IMPORTANCE OF 'LOCAL'

Local as personal identity

2.14   Geographers have always found it extremely difficult to define 'rural'. In the late 1970s, Paul Cloke developed a sophisticated 'index of rurality' which many found extremely helpful. Today, however, academics (including Cloke) have come round to the conclusion that in the last resort the way to discover whether a place is 'rural' or not is to ask those who live there! They have come to perceive that any definition of 'place' has a 'gut' content for each individual.

2.15   It is a commonplace that human beings seem to need to be rooted into a place (or places) if they are to be fulfilled and sane. The walls that surround are also the walls that support. In his lecture 'English Local

History, the Past and the Future', W. G. Hoskins quotes the planning theorist Lewis Mumford:

> Men are attached to places as they are attached to family and friends. When these loyalties come together one has the most tenacious cement possible for human society. In the restless movings about of the first two centuries this essential relation between the human spirit and its background was derided, under-estimated, sometimes overlooked. Where men shifted so easily, no cultural humus formed, no human tradition thickened.

2.16   The organization Common Ground has done much to highlight the importance of 'the place that is unique to me'. Individuals have been encouraged to identify those places which are most significant for them, and to explain why this is so. Local people then put together a 'unique places map' of their area. (Some of the most interesting work has been done with old mining 'villages' who have lost, and are trying to rediscover, their identity.)

2.17   One of the problems is, of course, that most of the 'places that are unique to me' are embedded in childhood memory. But the landscape we remember has changed, and so for most of us our unique place is already past history. We may be forgiven for being angry that our favourite childhood picnic spot is now part of the Winchester bypass – but is it really the present owner's fault that the garden wall we remember as six feet high is in fact a mere three feet? Devotion to the local place often ends up being very conservative indeed.

Local as defence mechanism

2.18   In the last few years anthropologists have helped us to see some of these issues with new eyes. Anthony Cohen has published an important study of Shetland society. He shows, first, that what looks to the outsider like a homogeneous, even tribal, community is in reality a very mixed group – an amalgam of many varied communities, albeit within one physical space. Far from behaving as one happy family, different groupings compete – not to say fight like cat and dog on some occasions. However, when faced with a 'threat' from outside, they rally around their common local identity. By 'threat' Cohen means anything from a visit by an individual from the mainland, to an armed invasion by enemy troops.

2.19   Paul Milbourne did a similar study of a deep rural area in Wales. He also found that in response to 'foreign threat' local people go out of their way to emphasize their stereotypical Welshness – Welsh language, singing, rugby, agricultural associations etc.

2.20   'Local' can mean a variety of things to the same person depending on the current 'threat' the individual is facing. For a Mancunian born and bred, when at home in a Manchester suburb, 'local' may mean 'those who live in my cul de sac'; when out for an evening in the city it could mean 'those who live in our suburb'; when working in Chester it might mean 'those who live in Manchester'; when in Bristol 'those who live in the North'; while when on holiday in Corfu, 'local' is England.

2.21   Arguably it is also the case that the further away from home we are, the less we are likely to be tied to reality and are, on the contrary, more and more influenced by stereotypical media images. The tone-deaf Welshman on holiday in New York is likely to argue that 'the Welsh love music'; while the suburban Yorkshire couple from an anonymous housing estate on the outskirts of Leeds find themselves agreeing that every northern town is a 'Coronation Street' community.

2.22   Today, therefore, many academics would argue that 'local' has a key importance for normal human development – both in terms of identity and of 'defence'.

A local lifestyle persists

2.23   It is also being recognized that the social space of most people is still very local. A family may absorb global images from the media, they may holiday abroad (though with the speed of travel there is usually such 'time-space compressions' that the contrasts are significantly blurred), they may even move to another region in search of a job, but for at least 90 per cent of the time the physical space they inhabit is extremely limited. Their experience of 'images' may be global, but their experience of 'reality' is still relatively local.

2.24   This is seen in the inevitable difficulties of a family moving house from one region to another. The main wage earner may enjoy a measure of social continuity, but for those, such as teenagers, whose access to a car is limited, the move is traumatic. From day one they have to establish a new series of networks to cover every aspect of their lives. They recognize with sickening clarity the continuing reality of geographical locality.

2.25   There is also new evidence that many more people have begun to work from home for at least part of their working week. The establishment and use of tele-cottages is just one outward and visible sign of the way modern technology is making it possible for businesses to operate again in villages – and even 'dormitory' suburbs.

2.26   We conclude that, on balance, the Church is right to continue to concentrate on 'the local'. Despite new technology and shared global images, most people still live very local lives. They value their local place, both because it keeps them sane, and because it defends them against threat from 'outside'. A strategy for mission which starts with 'the local' is a strategy which starts where most people are.

Some implications for LNSM

2.27   On the other hand, no mission strategy for the next century dare end there. The local church needs first to be aware of the complexity of 'local' life outlined above: that both 'local' and 'community' mean something different for each individual.

2.28   Secondly, there are very practical implications for the choice of a 'local' priest. Priests 'from outside' inherit a 'role' which relates to the whole physical space of the settlement. They inevitably give a personal emphasis to the role – but they remain a role figure, able to cross social space boundaries. Not so the 'local' priest who will be meshed into one of the many communities coexisting within the physical space of the settlement. Inevitably the local priest is not therefore 'local to the whole settlement' – and ordination will consequently throw up a host of personal problems for the individual, their family and others living in the village.

2.29   Thirdly, we would argue that the current situation positively demands that a local individual priest be part of a local team. Further that all the 'communities' within the settlement participate in the nomination process; and that so far as possible the members of the team are drawn from different groupings. This is especially true if the church is no longer an accepted local 'focus' (as in many urban situations), but is felt to be just one 'club' among many others.

2.30   Fourthly, the local church needs to reinforce the importance of the benefice and the diocese. As we saw for all of us today 'local' can sometimes refer to 'locality' (benefice), and sometimes to 'region' (county). By ensuring firm links with benefice and diocese the local church is underpinning 'reality' – and is guarding against false (sentimental) 'localism'.

2.31   Fifthly, understanding the social mechanisms of a local community will help the local team and local priest to be realistic when setting goals. They will not for instance expect 'everyone in the area' to support any one initiative (as might have been the case in the past). Nor will they be angry or feel undermined if many young people (whose preferred social space will usually be wider than the settlement) are catered for by the big church in the local market town (or even by the neighbouring 'community church').

2.32   Sixthly, the local church needs to be aware of the danger of the enculturation of 'local'. We suspect that that wily evangelist St Paul would tell us there is no harm in starting where people are – provided that we are determined to move further forward rather than to sell out to the purveyors of aspic.

15

A theological perspective on local

2.33   If we now return to the 'theological re-valuing of the local congregation' referred to at the beginning of the last section, it is clear that a
theology of 'local' must have its roots in the natural instinct of humankind
to reverence special places to which – as we have seen – anthropologists,
sociologists and geographers all bear witness.

2.34   The earliest layers of the Old Testament are probably traditions
which attach to particular holy places: and the fiercest censorship of the
final editors cannot hide the fact that most Israelites could not be persuaded to abandon their local holy shrines with their local priests in favour
of the Jerusalem Temple. Walter Brueggemann's pioneering work, *The
Land*, sheds light on the way in which the ownership of a particular piece
of land with clearly defined boundaries gave an individual their place as
one of the chosen people.

2.35   Jesus is for all people and all times. But he was also 'historical'.
He lived at a particular time in a particular place – Nazarene, Galilean,
Jew, a subject of the Roman Empire. Thanks to the work of modern schol-
ars, we are only now beginning to re-discover the importance of that
context for the formation of Christian tradition.

2.36   Pilgrimage to the places made holy by association with Jesus
appears to have been part of Christian devotion from the earliest years.
Clearly the experience of contemporary pilgrims of all the great faiths,
that for many one way to a closer encounter with God lies along a particular road which leads to a particular place, was part of the experience of
the earliest Christians too.

2.37   *Eucharistic Presidency*, a Theological Statement of the House of
Bishops of the General Synod includes a clear statement of the current
debate about the nature of the priesthood, which the authors believe
needs to be grounded in a theology of the church.

> A theology of the Eucharist, and an understanding of the
> respective roles of clergy and laity within it, need to be set
> within the wider context of a theology of the Church.

Approaching the theology of the sacraments and the theology of ordination in this way is rightly assumed in virtually all current writing on ministry and the sacraments, and in all recent major ecumenical documents on these themes. (2.1)

2.38   The statement points out that there has been a shift towards grounding the doctrine of the Church in the doctrine of the Trinity and draws attention to the contribution of Orthodox theologians to the debate. This section concludes:

While keeping in mind the pitfalls of correlating the Church and the Trinity we mentioned above, three relatively uncontroversial points about relationships within the Church may be registered at this stage. These are:

1.   There is no difference of worth before God.

2.   We must begin by thinking of our relatedness to each other:- only within this inter-relatedness will the identity of individuals and specific groups properly flourish.

3.   The Church is a community of persons-in-relation. (2.16)

2.39   Chapter three of the statement draws out the implications of these insights for the relation between priest and people and concludes that priests exercise their priestly ministry by virtue of their participation, with the whole body, in Christ's priestly ministry. The Anglican-Reformed Report, *God's Reign and Our Unity* states that:

'Priests' exercise their priestly ministry neither apart from the priesthood of the whole body, nor by derivation from the priesthood of the whole body, but by virtue of their participation, in company with the whole body, in the priestly ministry of the risen Christ, and as leaders, examples and enablers for the priestly ministry of the whole body in virtue of the special calling and equipment given them in ordination. (para 80) (3.25)

2.40   The relation of priest to people is made clear in the Eucharist when rightly understood. The statement twice quotes with approval words from the International Anglican Liturgical Consultation 195: 'In, through and with Christ, the Assembly is the celebrant of the Eucharist' (1.27). However, within the Assembly the priest has a special function 'which arises out of pastoral oversight. Separating liturgical function and pastoral oversight tends to reduce liturgical presidency to an isolated ritual function.'

2.41   The statement sees specific roles for the priest. First, that of pastoral oversight. This binds the priest to the local Assembly of which s/he is a member.

2.42   Secondly, 'the ordained ministry can be a means whereby the local is represented to the Universal Church and the universal to the local' (3.34). The statement also says,

> . . . those who are ordained do not stand apart from the Christian community; rather, those who are to be ordained are called from within the community and they are returned to serve within that community though serving in a new relation to it. This is not to be understood simply in terms of the community of a particular locality. From the earliest days of the Church, it appears that ministerial oversight both served particular congregations and held a number of congregations together in a wider communion of faith. He or she will also be licensed to exercise his or her ministry in a particular locality and within certain limits, thus giving expression in the local community to this ministerial relationship to the whole Church. But though this licensing is included in ordination it is not itself ordination. (3.29)

2.43   Thirdly, the priest is to be the guardian of the apostolicity of the Assembly:

We would suggest that, in relation to the people of God as a whole, the ordained ministry is best conceived as a gift of God to his Church to promote, release and clarify all other ministries in such a way that they can exemplify and sustain the four 'marks' of the Church – its oneness, holiness, catholicity and apostolicity. (3.26)

The calling of the priest to hold firm to the four marks of the church is underlined in the chapter on the Eucharist where the statement suggests:

. . . that the eucharistic president is to be a sign and focus of the unity, holiness, catholicity and apostolicity of the Church, and the one who has primary responsibility for ensuring that the Church's four marks are expressed, actualised and made visible in the eucharistic celebration. (4.45)

2.44   However, the priest is to perform these roles in the context of collaborative ministry. The statement sets out (3.11–19) how pastoral oversight developed in the early church and concludes:

A basic pattern of a pastor, a collegial association for the pastor, and pastoral assistants to carry out ministry in the world is one that has been adopted by the large majority of Churches in one form or another to the present day. In recent ecumenical discussion this has been expressed in terms of three dimensions of ministry: the personal, collegial and communal (synodical), exercised at the local, regional and universal levels of the Church's life. (3.16)

However, it is not clear that the threefold Anglican ordained ministry has always been practised in such a way that an appropriate balance has been struck between the three ministerial dimensions outlined in 3.16. The Reformed Churches, for instance, have expressed concern that in the Anglican tradition the personal dimension may become so dominant at times that it is isolated from the community and no longer exercised in relation to the responsibility of the synod. (3.19)

The Roman Catholic report *The Sign We Give* echoes many of these sentiments on behalf of its own church.

2.45   It may be useful to look sideways at how priesthood has developed in the Orthodox Churches. For them as for us, the understanding of priesthood is grounded in ecclesiology, and in their belief in the centrality of eucharistic worship.

2.46   In their understanding, the celebration of the liturgy is the supreme function of the priest and his other functions are in comparison insignificant. Indeed they are not so much 'functions' as 'charisms' which individual priests may have, but only if they are perceived to have them, will they be licensed to use them. Teaching and preaching are regarded as 'charisms' and by no means all priests are licensed to teach or preach.

2.47   All priests are seen as 'local' priests (the representative of one particular congregation), and they can neither celebrate the liturgy nor preach for any congregation except their own without the express permission of the bishop. While this is a matter of 'order', the theological reason for the regulation is that the liturgy is held to be true (valid) because of the worship of the congregation (assembly) expressed through their particular representative. Move either the priest or the congregation and the equation no longer balances.

2.48   Vocation to the priesthood may come initially through the call of God to an individual, or the call of a congregation to an individual. The fact that many priests are effectively 'pressed into service' is reflected in many Orthodox ordination rites. First, the part played by the congregation in signifying that they believe the ordinand to be 'worthy' is an essential part of the sacrament. Secondly, the ordinand approaches the bishop supported on either side by a priest – in case he may be tempted to try to run away!

The Anglican tradition

2.49   In its outline of the history of *Eucharistic Presidency* the statement points out (4.19–42) that early Anglican ordinals 'put considerable stress on the inseparability of ministerial office and the Church Community. This was brought out partly by the requirement (in the Preface to the 1550 Ordinal) that candidates for ordination be duly tried and tested, partly by their public interrogation by the bishop, and partly by the requirement that ordinations should be 'upon a Sunday or holy day, in the face of the church.'

2.50   Anglican priests have never been 'local' in the orthodox sense, but in practice many clergy returned to minister in the parish in which they were born. For instance the Leir family were Rectors of Ditcheat in Somerset, father and son for 256 years.

2.51   We as a Reformed Church differ from the Orthodox in our expectation that priests will be ministers of word as well as sacrament. But even in this respect practice did not always match the vision. Clergy were not always qualified to preach and often read homilies instead.

2.52   As Anglicans we have always valued the local place and the local congregation, and the fact that this is a central feature of our tradition is still very much evident today. The authors of *Church and Religion in Rural England*, much the most extensive survey of rural Christianity in this country ever carried out, reflecting on the evidence write as follows:

> It is easy to debate the nature of Anglicanism in terms of a three-fold order of ministry set amidst Prayer Book, the place of Reason in interpreting scripture, and Church Tradition. A better way of characterising the Church, however, might be in its parish organisation and ethos. The Parochial System con-stitutes the Church of England. It is the parish not the diocese, the priest and not the bishop, which forms the cen-tre of gravity of Anglicanism.

2.53   Of course things are changing, but in *The Clerical Profession*, Anthony Russell shows that clergy only came to regard themselves as a professional class in the early Victorian period. The 'invention' of theolog-ical education, the adoption of a distinctive dress, the re-ordering of churches and changes in the way services were performed all led to the raising of the clergyman and his family to a pedestal separating them from the rest of the local society. Initially (particularly in rural areas) many of these 'new' clergy served for most of their lives in the same parish and thus carved out for themselves a 'local' position (though a subtly different one from that of the predecessors): but this too has changed so that now it is unusual for a priest to remain in the same benefice for more than ten years.

2.54   Ronald Blythe, a perceptive commentator on the rural scene, writes in *Divine Landscapes*:

> The parish as a unit of landscape is the most associative contentious and distinctive personal region. It is venerated as the landscape of nativity and cursed as the landscape of limitation. Parish scenery pulls us this way and that, it is in control of us. Even the twist and turns of a city parish's streets have their special private direction for the born parishioner. In the country, where one can often see an entire parish from boundary to boundary, one can also often see one's entire life. It is comforting – and painful. For those who have remained in the same place a parish is not an address, it is somewhere you don't need one. But if one moves away after only a few formative years there is no severing the umbilical link that feeds one with its particular parochialism. One of the great difficulties experienced by a priest is that his flock never really understands that their parish can never be his – not in anything like the sense in which they possess it. Unless, as frequently happened at either end of Christian parish history, he happened to be a son of the village. Medieval farmer's son, Victorian squire's son, there is a BROKEN tradition of the local holy man taking charge of the local holy ground.

And of course the multi-parish benefice only exacerbates the break in the tradition.

2.55   What Blythe draws attention to is the fact that for most of

Christian history, and for much of English history too, there has been a close link between the local settlement, the local congregation and the local priest. 'Local' priesthood is not therefore a new invention, but it can perhaps be seen as a recovery of healthy rootedness.

Arguments against LNSM

2.56   We believe that there is a place within the ordained ministry for those whose ministry is 'local', but we are aware that there are arguments against it which are not in a narrow sense theological. Chief among those arguments is perhaps the fact that we live in a highly mobile society so the focusing on the local is simply misguided. We believe this criticism is partly answered by the fact that the average age of the 65 LNSMs who filled in the Questionnaire was 57 (see Section 4.8 of the report). In other words, these are people whose lives have reached a much more settled phase than those in mid-career in their thirties and forties. Evidence for this is that more than half (36) had lived in the parish in which they serve for more than ten years and that twenty were retired. If these were the only people being ordained they would, of course, be unrepresentative of the population at large but they have to be seen alongside the stipendiary and non-stipendiary ministry. Others conversely may want to argue that this average age of 57 is too high, but we believe that just as young Christians are helped by having young clergy as role models, so too older people can be strengthened and encouraged by their peers who have been ordained.

2.57   However, we are aware of variations between schemes in the average age of LNSMs. In the Manchester Scheme, for instance, LNSMs are, on average, 46 at the time of ordination. Whilst in general we would say that we live in a mobile society, it is clear that in some parts of the country this is less marked. In such places it may well be possible to identify people who, at a younger age, are, for a variety of reasons, unlikely to move from their locality.

2.58   Another objection that has been voiced is that the majority of people being ordained as LNSMs are classified as 'professional' (39 per cent) while another 19 per cent are seen to be managers or administrators, and that people from other backgrounds which it had been hoped would be attracted have not come forward. We believe these figures tell us a great deal first of all about the make up of an age profile of many of our congregations, but we would also point out that the largest group of LNSMs reported that they had left full time education at 16 or under. Other critics have argued that they can see no difference between NSMs and LNSMs. In some dioceses there is, in fact, a clear difference which is marked by deployability. In Truro, for example, NSMs will normally serve in a parish other than the one from which they came. In addition, in some dioceses NSMs become priests-in-charge of parishes. LNSMs are always seen as supplementary and complementary to an incumbent. In no case is it envisaged that they will have sole responsibility for a parish or benefice.

2.59 Then there are those who claim LNSM is ordination by the back door, or a soft option. The requirement of formal accreditation of LNSM schemes has ensured that this is not so. LNSM schemes are subject to the same requirements of accreditation and moderation by ABM as are theological colleges and courses. Accreditation is confirmed by the ratification of the House of Bishops and LNSM schemes are subject to regular inspection by the House of Bishops' Inspectors. This report makes recommendations about selection for training. Whether a conference is held locally or nationally, national criteria apply (see Section 5.19). But we also raise the possibility of Regional Conferences (5.22).

2.60 Clergy who do not follow this pattern of a full-time professional ministry, a career if you like, have been seen as inferior. Part-time, or unpaid ministers, ministers in secular employment, are often in church circles seen as 'amateur', helping out, filling in for the professional. Non-stipendiary ministry has been with us for a long time, but we still find evidence that it is seen as second best, a temporary measure, until universal stipendiary ministry may be restored. This feeling of inferiority has now been passed on to LNSMs, who are perceived by some as third rate.

2.61 A whole cluster of objections are focused around the issue of locality. Where selection and training is understood as local, it is seen as inferior to national selection and residential training. The emphasis on the need for LNSM schemes to be approved by the House of Bishops and for local selection to follow national guidelines helps to counter this. However, it is difficult to counter an argument of poor selection and training where diocesan schemes do not follow national guidelines and ordination takes place after only cursory training. Unfortunately some diocesan pilot schemes have done the general standing of LNSM a disservice by not taking selection and training seriously. When this has happened, it is difficult to refute the charge of 'ordination by the back door'.

2.62   A further criticism around the local issue is the simple question: 'How can a priest be local, when priesthood is catholic?' To restrict the exercise of priesthood to a particular locality appears to limit it in unacceptable ways. We have attempted to deal with this objection theologically in the theological perspective above. It is, though, important to emphasize here that the ordination of a local minister is the same ordination as any other. The area of ministry is, as for all clergy, limited by licence. However, the LNSM is selected and trained for a particular ministry in a particular place. Through their licence LNSMs are supported and encouraged by their bishop in focusing their ministry in that particular place. It is for this positive reason that they seldom minister outside the parish, even though, as priests of the universal church, they can naturally do so when it is desirable. The local licence may be seen as an acknowledgement of the importance of that ministry and a recognition that the significant difference in the mandate to the local priest is that he or she is not deployable in the way in which a stipendiary or non-stipendiary might be. This is neither better nor worse, just different.

2.63   Many lay people, including Readers and other authorized lay ministers, fear that LNSM adds another layer of hierarchy in the Church. On this understanding, the LNSM comes just below non-stipendiary and just above Reader in the parochial scheme of things and further marginalizes and undervalues the ministry of the 'ordinary' lay person in the pew. This criticism needs to be taken seriously. Careful selection is one of the ways of preventing status-seekers within a congregation becoming ordained. A proper recognition of the collaborative nature of LNSM described elsewhere in this report (see chapter 3) should help to break down the hierarchical perception of ministry. At its best it should release people for ministry and encourage them in it, whether accredited or not.

2.64   At a very practical level the criticism has been made that LNSMs may become stagnating influences in their parishes. Stipendiaries move on (or some of them do), but the LNSM, perhaps supported by an entrenched ministry team, could thwart any visionary or prophetic plans of an incoming stipendiary. This objection highlights the need for LNSMs to be engaged in continuing ministerial education (particularly, maybe, through occasional placements to see how things are done elsewhere), for the regular monitoring and review of local ministry teams where they exist, or the individual minister where they do not, and for the existence of LNSMs or teams to be taken very seriously where stipendiary vacancies occur.

2.65   One of the consistent objections to LNSM is its name. The title 'local non-stipendiary minister' could just as well be applied to a Reader, any accredited minister or any worshipping man or woman seeking to live out their faith in the community. 'Non-stipendiary' defines LNSMs by what they are not, i.e. paid, but fails to say what they are, i.e. ordained. Previous attempts at a title have failed. For example, 'local ordained minister' was seen by some to imply that the ordination may be local rather than catholic and therefore different. In practice we recognize that LNSMs locally are, like other clergy, called vicar, curate, priest, father, Christian name and so on. We recognize that a name is important. It is also useful for administrative purposes in distinguishing how many clergy are paid stipends and how many are deployable.

We recommend the title 'ordained local minister', which says what the person is and where he or she will minister.

CHAPTER 3

Collaboration

3.1   All Christians are called through baptism to share in the ministry and mission of the Church.

3.2   House of Bishops Regulations require that all LNSM schemes contain the following statement, or a statement consonant with it:

> Local Non-Stipendiary Ministry is part of the ministry of Christ which he shares with all baptized members of the church. Those called to this ministry by their local church need to have made the calling their own. For its effective operation, LNSM requires the local church's commitment to shared ministry, including the collaboration of local church leaders, ordained and lay. It is a development in ministry open to parishes and candidates of all social backgrounds.

3.3   As the statement makes clear, collaboration is at the heart of the development of shared ministry, a sharing between laity and clergy of their fundamental vocation arising from their baptism. LNSM grows from and is an expression of the shared ministry of Christians in a particular locality, setting apart, within the whole Church, certain men and women for the particular role of priest in that community, serving within a coherent team of clergy and laity.

3.4   We must be careful, when we reflect upon the vocation shared by all baptized members of Christ, that we do not interpret that vocation in a narrow and churchily-introverted way. The report *All Are Called* (Board of Education, 1985) spoke of that call that 'comes to us all, for all of our days and years, and for all of our activities' (p.3), and stressed that the call embraces ministries which are exercised in a church setting, ministries among family and friends, our 'Monday morning' ministries (i.e. within our secular occupations and involvements), our 'Saturday night' ministries (our leisure, sports, consumer activities). Too often, our developments in shared ministry have been narrow in interest, introverted and exclusive. Very often there has been a fundamental failure to engage with the real issues of peoples' lives, to support lay people in all layers and contexts of their lives. If the development of collaborative ministry fosters a narrow 'churchiness' then it is failing God and his people. We must be vigilant about this, because we know well that the true challenge and the true opportunity of collaboration is to foster a sense of corporate responsibility in our discipleship which will build up Christian communities which are able to support and release people to live out their vocation in all aspects of their lives.

3.5   Only in the light of a clear understanding of the vocation of the people of God can we go on to look at the nature of collaboration between clergy and laity, and to examine factors which help or hinder its growth.

3.6   As we have gathered evidence for this report we have become increasingly aware that collaboration requires some fundamental shifts of assumption and practice within the Church at all levels. To develop collaborative ministry at local level means that there must also be changes at all other levels. The following sections try to approach collaboration in terms of the attitudes, dispositions and commitments that are needed if collaboration is to begin, to grow and to flourish. What does it demand of people, of the Church (national, diocesan and local)? In particular we examine some of the issues of collaboration which are crucial to local ministry and LNSM.

3.7   It is usually clear when collaboration is absent in a parish (people are operating disjointedly, each somewhat isolated from others, often leaving it to the vicar), but how do we recognize it when it is present, or begin to develop it when it is largely absent. The identification of the signs and characteristics of collaborative ministry is a key task which faces all who are engaged in the development of local ministry and LNSM. Some have sought to list characteristics (cf. *A Time for Sharing*, pp. 48–9). Looking at the range of LNSM schemes, as well as at the wider picture of the development of local shared ministry, we can see that collaboration will include areas such as:

- a shared vision, with agreement about priorities and developments;

- commitment to spiritual nurture, corporate and individual clergy and laypeople sharing in the leading and planning of worship, sharing in decision-making and shaping of ideas;

- a consultative style of leadership at all levels;

- affirmation of a wide variety of gifts and skills;

- support of people in their daily lives beyond the gathered congregation;

- good communication between groups and individuals;

- continuing learning, corporate and individual;

- flexibility and openness to change, balanced with stability.

3.8   As we have received submissions and visited LNSM schemes we have been conscious of the wide variations in the ways that collaboration is practised and assessed. We have been aware of the differences that arise from the nature of the locality, and we have seen that what is possible and desirable in one setting may not be so in another. It is for this reason that we affirm the importance of each diocese thinking very carefully about the nature of the LNSM scheme best suited to its needs and vision. We have seen that difficulties arise when a diocese is tempted to adopt what is in essence an 'off the peg' scheme for LNSM, rather than undertaking the long and demanding task of working at the issues to discover the right scheme for itself. It is not a matter of 're-inventing the wheel' but a serious enterprise of audit, needs-assessment and theological reflection.

3.9   We have been aware, for example, of the differences in operating LNSM in urban, suburban and rural settings. If one compares the requirements of six scattered rural communities in one benefice in Lincolnshire with those of a small benefice in inner-city Manchester it is immediately apparent that a single model for LNSM will not do. If one adds the further settings of a market town in Herefordshire, an overspill estate on Merseyside and a suburban commuterland community in Guildford then the potential diversity is highlighted further. Flexibility in style, which nonetheless does full justice to a rigorous demand for genuine collaboration, will be essential if the potential of local ministries is to be realized.

3.10   There are many settings in which formally-constituted Local Ministry Teams (LMTs), nominated, trained and commissioned as a body, have great advantages. Among them are the experience of teamwork built up during training, the clear structural existence of a mutually supportive team, the opportunities for interdependence and complementarity among members, and the strength of continuity during periods of change (for example, between incumbencies). LMTs can help those who might otherwise be lacking in confidence to discover their unique gifts and potential, and can thus provide a secure yet challenging context for the ministerial development of a wide range of people. Likewise, those who might be more certain of their skills can learn the subtle art of contributing without dominating, and all can grow in a deep sense of service within the Body of Christ. LMTs have flourished in many parts of the country.

3.11   In the light of our earlier comments on the diversity of locality, however, we recognize that the formal LMT may not be appropriate in all settings. Two important examples will illustrate this:

(a)   There are parts of the country (often, though not always, urban) where a more flexible approach is required. In an inner-city parish, for example, where there is a small congregation, a high level of mobility (often through the development and re-development of council housing) and a high level of personal, social and economic pressures, it may be impossible to constitute and sustain a local ministry team with a stable membership. Nonetheless there may be a real commitment to collaborative ministry and there may be individuals who are able to be called to LNSM. A flexible approach is required if this local Christian community is to be supported and affirmed.

(b)   Some local churches have developed shared ministry over a considerable length of time. There may be one or two Readers, an established pastoral care team, a few people who share the responsibility for baptism preparation, a worship committee. In such a setting, the setting-up of an LMT for joint training may give all the wrong messages, seeming to devalue what already exists, including the training and experience of a wide circle of people. In many parishes of this kind, clergy and diocesan training officers will wish to be careful not to act as though there were a vacuum waiting to be filled, but rather to build carefully and flexibly on what already exists.

3.12   In both these cases clear and proven teamworking and a less formally constituted local ministry team will be appropriate. This will require very careful monitoring, and any diocesan scheme for LNSM with such flexibility must demonstrate the adequacy of the structures for regular review and appraisal of each parish, to ensure that collaboration is genuinely and pervasively present in the life of the parish. Such an 'organic' model places great demands on all concerned. It is essential that the PCC in such settings takes a full responsibility for the continuing development of collaborative ministry.

3.13   Dioceses with schemes for local ministry and LNSM, whether they use the model of formal LMTs or have a 'mixed economy' of formal and less formal local ministry teams, will need local ministry officers who can give close attention to the ongoing development of parishes. Any development of local ministry requires careful fostering and review. It also requires a consistent application of established diocesan policy at all levels, from bishops and archdeacons to area/rural deans, diocesan boards and committees, and clergy and lay leaders at all levels, from diocesan to local. If collaboration is truly to be nurtured in a diocese then all involved must quite literally practise what they preach.

The demands on incumbents and other stipendiary clergy

3.14   We have been aware throughout our work on LNSM of the key role of the incumbent in the development and maintenance of collaborative ministry. The more that shared ministry flourishes, the greater the demands on the stipendiary clergy. As the ministries of laypeople evolve and diversify, the stipendiary clergy have the extraordinarily complex task of exercising a leadership which is positive yet not autocratic, which encourages devolution and subsidiarity yet holds together a clear vision. At a time when stipendiary clergy are often uncertain of their own role in a changing Church and society, we are also asking them to undertake the task of being leaders and enablers of a new kind of collaboration. Is it not surprising that many stipendiary clergy feel ill-equipped for this task, nor that at times this lack of confidence manifests itself in hostility towards LNSM. All stipendiary clergy, at every stage of their ministry, need to be learning the skills of collaboration, of teamwork and of a sharing of ministry which is quite distinct from the exercise of delegation. Above all, no one should now be coming to the end of initial ministerial training without having learned collaborative skills and without a thorough grounding in the theology and practice of collaborative ministry, including a clear understanding of LNSM. **We recommend that all training for stipendiary and non-stipendiary clergy should include an understanding of LNSM.**

3.15   Some of the key qualities needed in an incumbent who is to work collaboratively will include:

- being a good listener and enabler;

- being willing to act as guide, adviser and consultant rather than benevolent dictator or efficient delegator;

- being willing to share leadership in ministry;

- being willing to see ideas and policies, the fruit of his or her professional knowledge and experience, postponed or rejected;

- giving support and training, in particular to members of local ministry teams and group leaders;

- holding regular meetings with leaders for consultation and planning;

- through all of the above, maintaining the incumbent's own proper ministry of word and sacrament;

- continuing to learn and being willing to explore new ideas;

- understanding and accepting that collaboration is better, but is not usually either easier or quicker.

(List adapted from Manchester LNSM Scheme)

3.16   Stipendiary clergy moving from one incumbency to another are learning, but slowly, that their arrival in a new parish does not open a new book with a blank page. Rather, they must observe, listen and learn. They must see what the people of God have been doing in that place already, and discover what they can, through their own experience, gifts and perspective, offer to that continuing ministry.

3.17   The following quotations from the survey of LNSMs serve as cautionary notes:

A new priest-in-charge arrived

> with no experience of working with a Local Ministry Team . . . unwilling to learn from and build on our corporate experience. The result has been disastrous. Five excellent Team Members resigned feeling very hurt and disillusioned. A very large section of the congregation have left for similar reasons, and there is much bad feeling in the parish.

And another writes of his incumbent:

> Prefers to do everything himself. Expects to take the leadership of all groups, even when these groups have been 'lay led' before, and is very reluctant to delegate anything unless absolutely necessary or pushed by the groups.

The demands on LNSMs

3.18   LNSMs receive a call from their parish, further explored and endorsed by the wider Church, to ordained ministry in their own particular locality. The demands of that ministry are considerable. We should not make the mistake of suggesting that this is in any way a 'soft option'. Rather, the disposition, integrity, skills and staying-power required are of a high order. Those who are called to LNSM must undergo a significant change of role within their own community. They must be able to work within a consultative and collaborative framework. They must have theological, spiritual and personal resources to enable them to minister among people in their local community over long periods of time. They must be flexible yet help to sustain continuities. They must give leadership yet be responsible to the incumbent.

3.19   Because of their position as members of the local community they are in some respects seen as available and accessible to people in a particular way. One LNSM writes:

> Many people see me as a priest, but on their side or at their level.

This is a particularly interesting statement because it allows us to see some of the strength of LNSM as a ministry which is 'of the people'. It is quite clear that LNSM really does allow the Church to reach out in new ways, tapping into cultural networks and social connections which might otherwise not be touched. This has indeed been one of the great hopes for LNSM in inner-urban contexts: the schemes for LNSM in dioceses such as Manchester, Southwark and Liverpool seek to use the development of local ministry and the ordination of people of a wide diversity of backgrounds as a tool of mission and ministry in areas which have been little touched by the Church.

3.20   Our survey of LNSMs showed that, nationally, there is a rather narrow social and occupational range among LNSMs, although we know that within this there are variations between schemes. In the light of the hope that LNSM will genuinely be open to parishes and candidates of all social backgrounds (see the statement from the House of Bishops' Regulations quoted in paragraph 3.2) dioceses and schemes will wish to ensure that they are genuinely affirming and making possible the development of LNSM in a wide variety of settings.

3.21   As we have seen earlier in this chapter, all Christians are called to live out the gospel in every aspect of their daily lives. LNSMs, by virtue of their non-stipendiary ordained ministry, share with lay Christians the task of Christian witness not just in the local community but in the world of work. It would be quite wrong to assume that it is only NSMs in the broader category who are well placed to explore the pressures, opportunities and ethical questions that arise in the workplace, whereas LNSMs are people concerned more narrowly with the gathered Christian community. On the contrary, LNSMs will be well placed, within the local church, to share with others in reflecting upon how people are to be supported in their wider lives and how best the local church may give proper space and attention to such issues.

Some legal and structural issues

3.22   Ministerial developments within the Church of England raise some special issues. In particular, we need to be very clear about the relationship between Local Ministry Teams (formal and organic) and Parochial Church Councils. We know that there have been instances of tension between them and that this can undermine or even destroy collaborative developments. Clarity about areas of responsibility and authority is essential. **We recommend that where a diocese develops Local Ministry Teams, the guidelines must clearly spell out the relationship with the PCC and must state clearly that it is the PCC with the incumbent which carries the legal responsibility in the parish.** This is also an important training issue, and members of Local Ministry Teams need to be clear about the relationship with the PCC.

3.23   Some areas of disquiet have arisen over the exercise of responsibility during a vacancy. What is the relationship between the area/rural dean, churchwardens and PCC and a commissioned Local Ministry Team? How are responsibilities to be decided upon and allocated? Bearing in mind the particular legal responsibilities of the sequestrators, there is some need for investigation of possible regulations which would clarify the position and avoid difficulties.

Relationships with bishops, senior staff and the appointment of stipendiary clergy

3.24   The development of LNSM has accelerated over recent years. In 1983 there were four diocesan schemes approved by the House of Bishops. Half way through 1997, there were fourteen. This indicates that a number of dioceses were exploring the possibility of LNSM at the same time, sometimes for different reasons, envisaging that this development would form a significant part of a strategy for ministry. It seems to us that local ministry will best succeed and be fruitful in the context of an overall diocesan strategy for ministry. Occasionally this has not happened and has led to the marginalization of those engaged in training LNSMs or of local ministers themselves. We want to affirm the diversity of approaches taken by individual dioceses as they explore LNSM and **we recommend that each diocesan submission to the House of Bishops should contain a rationale for wanting a LNSM scheme, and set it within the context of a diocesan strategy for ministry.** Part of the feeling of marginalization referred to above has come about from a feeling among some that once a diocese has a scheme, those at the centre of the diocese have lost interest or not made connections with other forms of ministry.

3.25   LNSM schemes are set up within dioceses as part of their overall ministerial strategy. In some cases there have been pressing circumstances which have made diversification of ministry essential, for example in rural situations where the amalgamation of benefices has made it necessary to find new ways of maintaining a ministerial presence in small villages. More broadly, though, LNSM has emerged from the development of collaborative ministry and the desire, for theological as well as pragmatic reasons, to build up ministry in ways which relate more closely to local situations. Whatever rationale pertains in particular dioceses, the coherence of LNSM with the diocesan pastoral strategy is a key underlying foundation for any LNSM scheme.

3.26   That being the case, the relationship between the scheme and the diocesan bishop and his staff is crucial for the operation. The practice of local ministry which is collaborative depends heavily on the support and the goodwill of the bishop. Only so can the continuity in the style of the stipendiary ministry which, on behalf of the bishop, oversees LNSM be maintained. Without that continuity, collaborative ministry and the specific ministry of the LNSM can be seriously undermined or collapse altogether. More broadly, the whole development of LNSM within the totality of ordained ministry demands large shifts in consciousness and practice.

3.27   Because LNSM schemes are concerned with the development, training and maintenance of those who are ordained as well as those who are exercising lay ministry, they need to have, and to be seen to have, a close working relationship with the bishop. Bishops themselves, particularly if they come to a diocese after the establishment of a LNSM scheme, need to understand it thoroughly, and to know what its existence means in practice for the oversight and the deployment of stipendiary ordained ministry. The scheme itself needs to be closely in touch with the policies and thinking of the diocesan senior staff. The relationship is thus a more complex one than the relationship which the governing body of a course or college has with any diocesan bishops. A recent Inspectors' Report on a scheme recommends that a suffragan bishop should be an ex officio member of the Local Ministry Committee (the governing body). This would seem to be a sensible way of ensuring that the relationship is maintained effectively, and **we recommend that a suffragan bishop (or in dioceses with no suffragan, a member of the bishop's senior staff) should be an ex officio member of the governing body of a LNSM scheme.**

3.28   Within the overall relationship with senior staff, the appointment of incumbents to parishes where there is, or is likely to be, LNSM is of critical significance. We must accept that there are many pressures and considerations which enter into the appointment of incumbents. Nonetheless, if a diocese has a scheme for LNSM it has a clear obligation to take the greatest care in the making of appointments and a clear duty to work with private patrons to ensure that they understand the nature of the collaborative ministry which underpins and characterizes LNSM.

Earlier experience with lay ministry teams of various kinds, including UPA teams such as those set up under GUML (Group for Urban Ministry Leadership) in Liverpool, has shown how fragile collaborative ministry is in the face of a hostile or apathetic new incumbent, and also how hard it can be to hear what a prospective incumbent is really saying in response to questions about shared ministry.

3.29   Time and again during our work we have heard of instances where collaborative ministry has been fatally undermined by the making of an inappropriate appointment to the incumbency. It is impossible to stress too much the importance of diocesan bishops and their senior staff exercising the greatest care in this area.

3.30   We are aware of the many pressures on bishops in the making of appointments, of the variety of factors to be taken into account, and of the relative paucity of candidates in some cases.

However, we make the following recommendations in relation to local ministry in the hope that future problems may be minimized.

(a)   **The diocesan bishop should have unequivocal evidence of a prospective incumbent's commitment to shared ministry, and be sure that it is not merely a commitment to delegation.**

(b)   **The papers describing the parish should state clearly the present nature of collaboration in the parish and include information about any existing Local Ministry Team and LNSMs (either already ordained or in training).**

(c)   **The prospective incumbent must meet any LNSMs in the benefice (ordained or in training) and the LNSM(s) must be given the opportunity to make their views known to the bishop before any offer is made.**

(d)   **Where there is an established and commissioned Local Ministry Team, or one in the course of training, it must be made clear to the prospective incumbent that this is**

a 'given' in the parish.

(e) **New appointees should undergo training in the diocese before moving to their new post, and must commit themselves to ongoing training.**

3.31   We realize, of course, that given freehold and other legal constraints our recommendations cannot prevent all problems. We do believe, however (and experience in LNSM schemes bears this out), that where diocesan senior staff really do commit themselves to this kind of good practice the occasions of bad appointments can be minimized. In virtually all the bad cases of which we have heard, attention to the above points was either missing or inadequate.

3.32   Appointments of other stipendiary clergy also need to be made with care in relation to LNSM. It cannot be assumed that all stipendiary curates, for example, will work collaboratively. There are instances where serious problems have arisen with the arrival of a new curate, sometimes because of lack of training in collaborative ministry, sometimes because of hostility to the concept of LNSM, sometimes because of confusion about areas of responsibility. It has to be remembered that a newly ordained stipendiary deacon has a huge adjustment to make in settling into his or her ordained ministry, getting to know a new area and new people, and learning a whole series of new roles and responsibilities. An established LNSM, known, settled and widely respected can seem a very considerable threat in such circumstances. Great care in the choice of training incumbents and parishes for new stipendiary curates can, however, make the parish which has developed collaborative ministry and LNSM an ideal place for the early training of stipendiary clergy.

3.33   In our survey of LNSMs we heard of very mixed experiences.

> I have not undergone a course of training in a theological college, so someone like me is perceived as watering down the traditional priesthood.

It is the clear responsibility of bishops to ensure that inappropriate appointments of team vicars and assistant clergy are not made, and that there has been ample opportunity for new appointees to receive training.

Parishes with LNSMs and LMTs as training parishes

3.34   We affirm the value of using parishes with good established collaborative ministry as training parishes for newly ordained stipendiary and non-stipendiary clergy. A solid experience of collaborative ministry, with a diversity of clergy and laity exercising ministry together, and a firmly-established framework of ministerial team working, will prove an invaluable start in the exercise of ordained ministry. The serving of titles within such parishes should become the norm.

3.35   It is important that the diocesan pastoral committee is fully informed about LNSM since the decisions it may make can have a huge impact upon local development. The changing membership of the pastoral committee makes it difficult to ensure that all members are equally well acquainted with the principles of LNSM, so here too the senior staff have a key role.

3.36   It is essential to the positive development of LNSM that it forms a coherent part of diocesan strategy and that staff at all levels work in accordance with that strategy. Accurate information about LNSM is essential, and the work of LNSM officers and principals or Local Ministry officers in ensuring that adequate understanding exists is vital. However, the promotion of understanding of LNSM should not be left to LNSM staff, as though it were their task to 'sell' LNSM. If LNSM really is part of the diocesan strategy, then the senior staff will make it their business to ensure that LNSM is understood to be a 'given' in the diocese, not a minority hobby. **We recommend that LNSM officers and principals have regular access to senior staff meetings.**

3.37   The diocese of Southwark has produced some useful notes for those involved in making appointments in relation to shared ministry:

Appointments in parishes where there is a pattern of shared ministry, a ministry for mission team, or a local non-stipendiary minister (LNSM)

NOTES FOR THOSE INVOLVED IN MAKING APPOINTMENTS

The appointment of a new incumbent in a parish where there is a commitment to shared ministry and team working is crucial to the effective working of the parish. Local non-stipendiary ministers are ordained on the understanding that their ministry will be exercised within a parish in the context of a shared or collaborative style of ministry. Experience suggests that the time following the appointment of an incumbent is the most critical point in the life of a team or the ministry of a LNSM.

But what is shared ministry? Shared ministry is about every Christian being called to share in God's ministry in the world. This leads to shared leadership within a congregation where the aim is to free the gifts of all the baptized for service in Christ.

In order to illustrate what we mean, here is an example of styles based on a hypothetical ministry to those who are housebound or sick in a parish. All these styles may be evident in a person's ministry but for effective working with a team, the ability to minister in the collaborative or enabling model is absolutely essential.

- 'individual' – incumbent visits a sick parishioner

- 'advisory' – incumbent gathers people together who reflect on the needs of the sick

- 'delegated' – incumbent asks a parishioner to go and visit a sick person and report back to him/her

- 'collaborative or shared' – team and incumbent decide who is the appropriate person to visit and share reflections on the visits

- 'enabling' – parish visitation ministry is administered by the team or parishioners.

There is a need for a person who can take the initiative but is not overly competitive or arrogant. When asking questions about past ministry, look for the word 'we' rather than 'I'. One of the main misunderstandings which people have is in the area of 'shared' and 'delegated' authority.

Many clergy look upon a host of people doing a multitude of jobs and reporting back as shared ministry. The incumbent with this style of 'delegated' authority can have an enormous amount of control over a congregation. This can be a major source of frustration and anger in a team where decisions, policy and reflection on issues have taken place in a team setting. An enabling ministry is creative, but just to make sure that the candidate is an enthusiastic worker and not a shirker:

Look for someone who:

1. Can share faith – the ability to be open about one's faith is essential for good team working.

2. Can show how they have worked creatively with others in past ministry or employment.

3. Is secure in his/her sense of self. A sign of spiritual maturity is when people are secure enough to help others develop their gifts beyond their limitation. An incumbent in a context of shared ministry needs to be capable of dealing with conflict, loss and criticism, while being aware of his/her own vulnerability and weakness.

(Southwark Diocese)

CHECKLIST FOR GOOD COLLABORATIVE MINISTRY

How to recognize it when you see it!

3.38   There will be:

- prayer;

- shared purpose, aims and objectives;

- a high level of communication, not only within the church congregation but also between the church and the community;

- a high level of trust and tolerance;

- team meetings involving clergy, Readers and lay leaders;

- input into the life of the church from all directions, not a reliance upon the faithful few;

- evidence of people valued;

- mutual enablement;

- wide recognition of skills and limitations;

- flexibility;

- openness to change;

- allowing initiatives;

- evidence of consultation and shared decision taking;

- desire for growth in understanding;

- a desire to do more;

- a similar quality of input from lay people into church as into work;

- lay people involved in pastoral work and for this to be acceptable within the parish;

- a ministry of welcome involving clergy and lay people;

- lay participation in worship and planning worship;

- clergy who do not attempt to fill every breach in times of crisis;

- some form of accountability and appraisal of those ministries;

- space and scope for personal growth, including staff development and professional growth;

- productive ways in which the Body heals itself, including agreed conflict resolution procedures.

(Adapted from Board of Mission, *A Time for Sharing*, 1995)

CHAPTER 4

The current situation

4.1   As part of our research we visited over half of the approved LNSM schemes and received written contributions from all of them. Different dioceses identified a variety of reasons for wanting a scheme. These ranged from a desire to fill gaps left by decreasing numbers of stipendiary clergy, through to a perceived need to move parishes towards every member ministry. Every member ministry soon opens up the need for representative ministry. As the exercise of priesthood is bound up with a local congregation, so each local congregation needs a sacramental person who is 'theirs'. Both of these approaches acknowledge the importance attached to the presence of an ordained person as part of a local Christian community. In rural dioceses, for example, particularly in multi-parish benefices, the emergence of the local non-stipendiary priest has once again offered the possibility of local pastoral and sacramental care in a way that seemed to be a thing of the past when such geographically large benefices were established. In this case the development of LNSM may be seen to be truly radical in that it returns to the root understanding of Anglican ministry.

4.2   In conversation with LNSM officers, principals and candidates, the following practical reasons for wanting an LNSM scheme emerged:

- One diocese identified a need for more priestly hands, particularly in places with large congregations, so that local priests could be slotted in to existing teams.

- One diocese wanted a priest for every place and congregation; teams could come later.

- Several dioceses were clear that ministry teams should come first. From these teams potential ordinands might emerge. Generally among these dioceses (particularly in urban areas) emphasis was put on the development of an indigenous ministry.

- Several dioceses sought substantial evidence of collaborative or shared ministry in a parish before consideration could be given to the identification of a potential LNSM.

- Others were prepared to identify a candidate and build a team around him or her.

4.3   We are happy to affirm a diversity of approaches given that the needs of different dioceses vary, as do the circumstances of individual parishes and groups of parishes. However, there needs to be a rigorous examination of the context for local ministry. We were persuaded that collaborative or shared ministry should be confirmed as a necessary mark of LNSM (cf. ABM Policy Paper No. 1 pp.10–11). If LNSM is seen or understood as plugging gaps or ministry on the cheap, it will deserve to fail. If it is seen as a call to all that is best about an ecclesiology of the Body of Christ, and a complementarity of gifts then it will stand in its own right and inform the ministry of the whole Church.

THE MARKS OF LNSM

The continuum

4.4   One way to visualize the process is to picture a continuum line between 'all clerical' and 'all member' ministry. Various models of ministry slot in at different points on the continuum, and most parishes will progress along the line over a period of years. The inference we need to draw from the diagram is, not that one model is superior to another, but that anything is good and valuable providing that it is moving in the right direction.

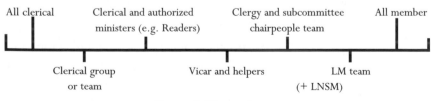

Figure 1: The continuum.

4.5   Managing a change of this nature is not going to be easy or swift. Business consultants suggest that to change cultural norms takes years rather than months; and we should not therefore expect overnight miracles. It is the role of the clergy which is at issue, and it is the clergy who are expected to lead the way. Clearly both stipendiary ministers and LNSMs will need professional training in how to manage this change both in the parish and within themselves. The development in the style of leadership to be exercised by the priest is represented in the following diagram.

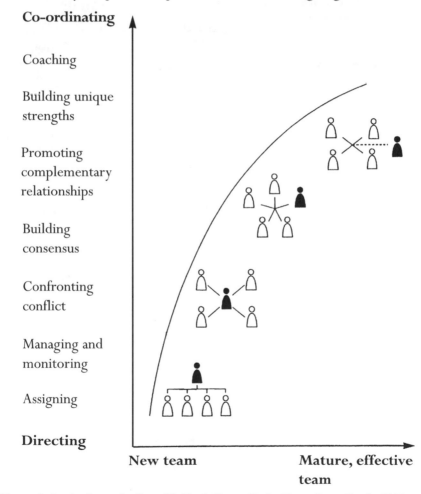

Figure 2: Leadership style, from *Workbook: How to Head a Team*, CareerTrack, 1996.

4.6   After ten years of experience we felt that the context, characteristics and competencies appropriate for LNSM can now be discerned. The following chart may help set these out.

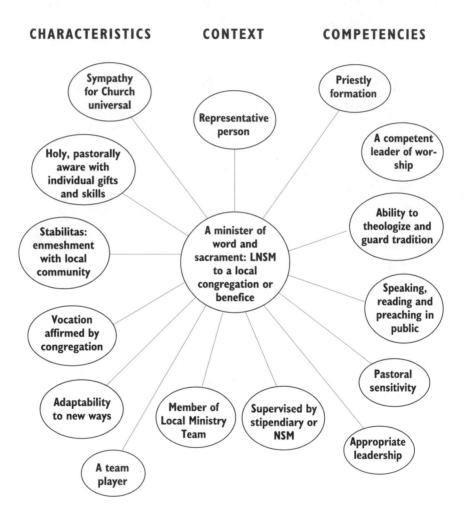

Figure 3: The context, characteristics and competencies appropriate for LNSM.

THE SURVEY

4.7   The survey on Local Non-Stipendiary Ministry commissioned by the Working Party gives a clear picture of the current situation of LNSM during the latter part of 1996. The questionnaire that was used can be found in Appendix 3 (see p. 104). The following is a summary of the survey's findings and allows LNSMs to speak for themselves.

Social profile of the LNSM

4.8   The rapid development of LNSM is confirmed by the fact that 46 out of the 65 respondents were ordained from 1993 onwards. The largest group of the respondents described their churchmanship as central (twenty-five) with fifteen open evangelical, nine modern catholic, eight conservative evangelical and four traditional catholic. The average age of all the respondents was 57.

4.9   Forty-seven respondents live in the benefice in which they minister and seventeen reported that they lived just over the parish boundary or in a nearby town. Of those who live in the benefice 36 have lived there for more than 10 years. Sixty of the sixty-five respondents have access to a car. Sixty-one of them live in owner-occupied housing, one reported their housing as privately rented and one rented from the Council.

4.10   Twenty out of sixty-five (31 per cent) reported that they have a degree. The largest group reported that they had left full-time education at 16 or under. At ordination 30 were in full-time paid employment, 10 in part-time paid employment and 20 were retired. At the time of the survey those numbers had changed to 24, 12 and 24 respectively. Of the occupations that were classified, 39 per cent (22) were defined as professional occupations and 19 per cent (11) as managers and administrators. The dominant single occupational category was the teaching profession (15 out of the 22 professionals were teachers or headteachers, etc.).

The benefice and its staff

4.11 Respondents were asked to give numbers of benefice staff. Forty of sixty-five benefices have one stipendiary clergy person, and fourteen have two. Twelve out of sixty-five benefices have five non-stipendiary staff and eleven benefices have three of them.

4.12 Twenty-two out of fifty-nine (who answered the question) have one staff meeting a month, twenty-one have more than three a month. Six did not answer the question as posed, but although 'none' was not offered as an option, four indicated that they did not have any staff meetings.

Comments included:

- None! It's appalling.

- We have a system where services are booked between us all and indicated on a sheet. No staff meetings take place at all.

- They are held during the day, not sure how often . . . I'm not invited.

4.13 Fifty-five respondents identified themselves as part of a ministry team: eleven as a team ministry, three as a group ministry, nineteen as a formal local ministry team, and seventeen as an informal local ministry team. When asked about how their role might differ from that of other members of the team several noted that they carry out the priestly duties which laity cannot do and thus have a role as the incumbent's 'second in command'. A few make special mention of conducting services, preaching and teaching. However, pastorally orientated roles are more common such as bereavement support, sick visiting, preparation for baptism. In some cases there is specialization by virtue of 'localness' e.g. local pastoral knowledge and continuity, and an emphasis on availability.

Services

4.14 Respondents were asked how often they preach in a month. Ten said once, twenty-one said twice, eighteen said three or four times, four said five or six times and two said seven or eight times.

Seventeen out of fifty-nine respondents answering celebrate the Eucharist twice a month in their benefice. Others range from once to six times.

During the last year thirty-one respondents baptized one to five people, ten respondents baptized six to ten, and eleven respondents baptized more than ten people.

In the same period nineteen respondents married between one and three couples, ten married four to six couples and five married more than six couples.

In the same period twenty-nine respondents officiated at the funerals of between one and five people, eight respondents at between six and ten, and fourteen respondents at more than ten.

4.15   Respondents were also asked to indicate, for the last year, the number of services taken outside the benefice. Thirty-five out of sixty-four had taken at least one service outside the benefice but within the deanery. Sixteen had taken a service outside the deanery but within the diocese. Thirteen had taken a service outside the diocese.

4.16   Two respondents commented upon the restriction placed upon LNSMs taking services outside their own benefice:

- As a Reader I was allowed to minister in other parishes, now as an ordained person I can only do this with permission for something special. I find this difficult to accept.

- Although I am considered a 'proper priest' by the local clergy and congregation and was ordained alongside stipendiary clergy I find it difficult to explain why I am not allowed to accept invitations to lead worship on special occasions in other parishes.

Appraisal of the team

4.17   In response to the question 'Has your team and/or parish ever been appraised?' Twenty-two said 'yes' and forty said 'no'. Of the twenty-two, five had been appraised by the rural dean, and seventeen by 'other'.

In ten cases 'other' was the bishop, sometimes with a team, and in four cases, some form of diocesan team.

4.18   In some cases appraisal and outcomes focused on specific restructuring issues including LNSM.

- The appraisal was concerned with my own future role in the parish.

- By making various suggestions in their final report – for instance that it might become a united benefice.

- It helped the parish to identify the need for the selection and training of a LNSM.

4.19   General positive comments were:

- PCC learnt more about the work of the team; team given opportunity to question and speak their mind; also receive advice.

- Renewed mandate for Local Ministry Team. Gave the congregation a chance to speak.

- It highlighted the need for new members to be trained and for present members to make themselves better known to the congregation.

4.20   In several cases, appraisal was viewed negatively or seen to bring little benefit.

- Not sure (long time ago).

- Apart from one or two administrative points there was nothing else raised.

- Very little. When I think of HMI inspections in school, this one lacked depth and seriousness.

- Not sure it was 'appraisal' but full day official visit with written report to diocesan bishop. I wasn't involved in any of the preparation or discussion for it. I haven't been shown the report (I have asked).

Appraisal of Local Non-Stipendiary Ministry

4.21   A similar series of questions addressed appraisal of the respondents' own ministry. Twenty-seven respondents said that they had been appraised. Of these, twelve were by the incumbent, one by the rural dean and others by the bishop or LNSM coordinator/director. Thirty-five respondents said they had not been appraised and the same number said they would like to be appraised next year. Positive comments on outcomes included the role of appraisal in helping ministers to take stock of their current role and how they wanted to develop. In addition, appraisal was seen as playing an important part in encouragement and reassurance.

- Posed some questions about where I go next.

- Highlighted strengths and weaknesses.

- Helped to re-shape LNSM scheme.

- Reassurance. Guidance on reasonable amount of time to devote to parish duties. Discussion on post-retirement ministry.

The effect of ordination on a minister's personal life

4.22   Personal fulfilment.

Increased personal fulfilment was one clear message.

- I feel more 'complete' and fulfilled as a person.

- My ordination has been a 'togetherness' with many people involved and will, I think, remain that way.

- My life is much more fulfilling and I am very happy despite the trials and tribulations which occur.

4.23   Pressures.

The pressure of time available for their LNSM role is a significant concern for several respondents who are in secular employment. The following quotations point to the need for particular understanding and support from clergy and others to allow the LNSM to contribute.

- I spend more time in prayer – and less on the garden!

- Constraints on time available for recreation.

- More of a hectic existence. Spare time decreased considerably.

- I have to juggle my time very carefully between church work, daily work and time spent with my family.

- The pressure on time and on expectations not realized should not be underestimated. The task is carried out at the expense of leisure which becomes a scarce if not abstract idea.

- My day is busier, I need to plan time for family and myself and have firmer boundaries.

- Don't have enough quiet prayer time, and certainly don't read enough.

- Time is hard to find, there is need to be with my family, wife and a time to be alone.

- I enjoy being an LNSM but have found this to be very time consuming. I would say in my experience that being an LNSM in full-time employment is very demanding and tiring, and one can never achieve what one sets out to do, due to the time factor. A handicap to me is not having a study as such. My writing (sermons etc.) has to be done either in the dining room or kitchen or even in my bedroom. I find that distractions occur with this arrangement.

- Being in full time secular employment means that the time for parish work is limited and it can be difficult balancing time on formal parish business with study time, reading time etc.

- Usually LNSMs work full time and are therefore available evenings/weekends only. I am fortunate that I work part-time as a teacher and therefore have more time available during the day – although this varies from week to week depending on the supply work I do and requires a certain amount of flexibility. There have been several occasions when a church commitment has conflicted with the availability of work, but usually this is not a problem.

Effects on and of the family

4.24   While a small number of respondents indicated that ordination had had no impact on their family, most had some comment to make. Some respondents point to positive impacts on the family:

- It's made them think more about the Christian faith. They've become a little less dependent on me.

- [I am] A source of expert knowledge for family funerals; opens new topics of conversation on life issues.

- They feel a certain pride.

- They 'boast' of having an ordained auntie, sister-in-law etc. and bring questions from those who wouldn't normally ask them.

- Little, as a worshipping family we have enjoyed and continue to enjoy our life together.

- A beneficial effect. They are happy and proud about my ordination.

- We seem to be closer.

- They are all pleased for me and happy to see me fulfilled in this way.

- They have happily accepted it.

4.25   For a large number of respondents, pressure on time has created tensions in family life, though several also emphasized the importance of support from their family in allowing and helping them to manage time and achieve balance. A sample of the comments in this category are listed below.

- They now see less of me of course, and this does at times annoy them.

- It has caused tensions with my wife.

- At times there can be a clash of priorities.

- Family functions have had to be adjusted.

- Extra pressure, particularly in terms of time, has created some problems.

- My wife tends to resent the time I spend, e.g. on prayer – though she's happy to realize that I feel fulfilled.

- It's not the sort of retirement which my wife had had in mind but she very loyally indeed supports me in my ministry. So far as other members of my family are concerned, there is not all that much difference in their perception of me as a Reader – which I was for twenty-seven years.

- They see less of me on Sunday mornings. A period of adjustment to a different Sunday routine was required.

- They recognize that Sunday is a working day for me, but Saturday is family day, otherwise not really affected.

- A re-ordering of family priorities especially in time allocation.

- No great changes. Small things, e.g. having meetings at my home, telephone messages etc.

- Wife also ordained – some effect of 'working evenings' – need for good diary management and earmarking 'family evenings'.

- The telephone rings more often!

- They have become more co-operative in helping me co-ordinate the mix of roles, and more understanding.

- Less time for family but they recognize God has called us all to serve him in our own ways.

- There have been tensions within my marriage (and I have a strong one!). Husband coping with demands on my time. We manage to talk it through and accept that he can moan about it from time to time. He is a tremendous support and a practical safety net. He doesn't attend church.

Adjustments in work and community

4.26   Being ordained has, for some respondents, made them question their secular employment.

- I feel less satisfied in my 'bread and butter' job and feel that sometimes it gets in the way of improving and developing my ministry in the parish.

- I have had to reduce the amount of paid work that I do to accommodate LNSM work.

- I have changed my job to allow more time for parish work.

Some respondents note issues with respect to the minister's relationship to the community.

- Very little (effect on family). My husband is the local doctor so, as a family, we are used to being 'public property'.

- My wife is expected to be a 'vicar's wife' in the parish. I am not available for my children during their day.

- Being a priest at work, my colleagues now are somewhat guarded in their speech when in my presence.

- More 'visible' within the community in which I live.

- Community now fully accept myself and family in what they see as new roles.

- I have to be more careful about what I say/protect confidentiality, etc.

- I sometimes wish I had conversation other than 'church'.

The acceptance of Local Non-Stipendiary Ministry

4.27   Several questions explored the degree to which LNSM was accepted. Closed questions asked about perceptions of the LNSM as a 'proper priest', ability to attend meetings of the deanery chapter, access to the bishop and views of any new incumbent appointed.

4.28   These closed questions were asked:

Do you think your local community regards you as a 'proper priest'?

Do you think your local congregation regards you as a 'proper priest'?

Do you think the other clergy in your benefice regard you as a 'proper priest'?

Do you think the other clergy in your chapter regard you as a 'proper priest'?

	Yes	No	No other clergy in benefice	Not answered
Community	58	3		4
Congregation	60			5
Other clergy in benefice	56	5	3	1
Other clergy in chapter	49	9		7

4.29   Responses to the closed questions suggest that there may be some problems with acceptance. The nature and extent of the problems is revealed by respondents' comments, which were offered not just as illustrations for 'no' answers but also by those answering 'yes' or those not answering the question.

4.30   Do you think your local community regard you as a 'proper priest'?

- To a point.

- Most do, some do not.

- Because I have a profession as a teacher I am thought of as a lay-man.

- Yes, but often they still expect a visit from the vicar as well.

4.31   Do you think your local congregation regard you as a 'proper priest'?

- Yes and no. Most do but a few regard the rector as the proper one.

- Many local people see me as a priest but on their side or at their level.

- They generally refer matters initially to the incumbent. This might be a function of still being in secular employment.

4.32   These perspectives do not seem cause for alarm. Indeed in their general comments, some respondents made special reference to their place in, and support from, the community:

- It is a satisfying and, I believe, productive ministry. Of course having been here as the Head of the Primary School and a Reader at the church since 1970 has helped. The parishes 'called' me to do this work and after eight years I still retain their affection and support.

- Positive reaction of local community to my ordination – effect of 'localness' being valued and recognized. Although within local congregation time tends to obscure LNSM status as new members of church arrive – and only see 'priest' and not label!

4.33   More troublesome viewpoints are attributed to the question 'Do you think that other clergy in your benefice regard you as a "proper priest"?'

- Advised by one to change courses and become a proper priest.

- Vicar does not agree with LNSM theologically.

- Some do and some don't – I think they think we got in through the back door.

4.34 When it comes to chapter level, the theme of perceived inferiority comes over even more strongly. Several respondents answering 'yes' to the question 'Do you think the other clergy in your Chapter regard you as a "proper priest"?' still chose to qualify their answer:

- Yes: now, but it took a bit of working out, to begin with we were not invited to join chapter (but neither were NSMs).

- Yes: some of the other NSMs seem to regard me as 'slightly inferior'. If you take the deanery chapter (whose meetings I cannot attend), I have found all the clergy I meet willing to accept me on equal terms.

- Yes: I have heard (second hand) a couple of derogatory comments. But most clergy and all congregation members are very supportive.

4.35 The responses from these answering 'no' or not answering the question as posed, included the following :

- Not answered: the rural dean refers to me as a 'so-called priest' – NOT encouraging!

- Not answered: not from a good enough, professional academic background.

- No: I feel that they hold the view that we have not had 'proper' theological training.

- No: I am a full-time lawyer. Some priests, not all, appear to find it difficult to accept full-time occupation outside of Holy Orders.

- Not answered: stipendiary priests (some) feel threatened by the concept of LNSM: priests shall be priests and nothing else!

4.36   In response to the question 'Do you often find it difficult to attend meetings of the deanery chapter?', half answered 'yes' and half 'no'. In nearly all cases problems were due to timing with meetings usually scheduled during working hours. Sometimes, in the light of experience, more convenient meetings were being arranged.

The bishop

4.37   Respondents were asked two simple questions about the bishop. In answer to 'Do you feel you have the same access to the bishop as stipendiary clergy?' Sixty out of sixty-five answered 'yes'. In response to the question 'If the bishop sends a letter to all clergy, does your copy come directly to you or via a stipendiary?' All answered 'Direct.'

The incumbent

4.38   The role of the incumbent is central to the LNSM's experience:

- I would not have felt able to take on this responsibility without the total support and encouragement of a like-minded incumbent.

- The role of the incumbent is crucial to the success of an LNSM's life; my incumbent is excellent in providing training and support, encouragement and trust. At the same time he is very careful to ensure that I am not overloaded.

- Appointment of a vicar to our parish who was not in favour of LNSMs was a severe setback to constructive ministry on the part of my fellow LNSM and myself.

4.39   Thirty respondents had experienced a change in incumbent, and in twenty-two of these cases the respondent's advice on the appointment had been sought. To the question 'Do you think the new incumbent is comfortable with the principle of Local Non-Stipendiary Ministry?' Nineteen said 'yes' and six said 'no'. Among the comments received were:

- The ministry is not fully understood as being collaborative/shared and I don't feel it is accepted as a specific ministry. It is thought to be an 'unnecessary' ministry.

- He is used to being a 'one man band' and finds it difficult to adapt to working with a team. He feels threatened by, jealous of, undermined by, the gifts and talents of others and cannot make best use of them.

- [yes] Now. LNSM was beyond the ken of incumbent when he came; he needed – and needs – training for the situation.

- He is enormously supportive and affirming and treats me as a colleague.

KEY POINTS ARISING FROM THE SURVEY

4.40   In seeking a way forward for LNSM, the following general points should be noted.

First, respondents overwhelmingly reported LNSM as a very positive experience, bringing them great joy and happiness. The role of the LNSM as a community priest with special 'local knowledge' was viewed as a 'productive ministry'.

Secondly, the majority of respondents reported that they had had to make sacrifices in their personal lives. These were predominantly associated with pressures of time, especially for those in secular employment. This left some LNSMs feeling they fell short of their own expectations as to what they should be offering. Leisure time was also reduced. Pressure was placed on members of the family to whom the minister looked for support.

More specific findings are listed below, and raise interesting issues.

(a)   The social profile of LNSMs is quite narrow. No respondents are under forty. The great majority are men. A large number are in professional occupations or are managers and administrators;

teaching is the most frequently cited occupational category. Virtually all are owner-occupiers.

(b) In terms of roles within a team there seems to be some variety of experience. In some cases the LNSM is essentially 'first reserve' for the rector (for instance filling in during an interregnum), whereas in other cases there is a specialist role, for instance in pastoral support. This variety may reflect personal choice and strengths. However, in some cases it could reflect confusion within the team, contributing to frustrations as LNSMs are stretched across too many tasks – as a 'gap filler' or 'ecclesiastical polyfilla'.

(c) It is not always easy for LNSMs to meet with members of their teams, or with other members of deanery chapter. While this is usually due to conflicts of time, sometimes it seems they are not even invited to meetings. In some areas special arrangements have been made to make it easier for them to attend.

(d) Generally, the experience of appraisal is not very positive: a large number of teams/parishes had not been appraised, some respondents found it difficult to identify how it had helped, and a very few did not even know what it was. Although appraisal of the LNSM's own ministry is viewed more favourably, and seems to have been carried out more frequently (or at least more recently), there were still examples of respondents being unable to find anything positive to say about it.

(e) The majority of respondents had attended study days, and about a third had attended a residential course or regular course of several sessions over the last year. However, it is clear that in-service training is not always sensitive to the needs of LNSMs, especially those in employment who may not be able to attend at certain times.

(f) A small number of respondents mentioned issues of resources, that LNSMs have to pay for Continuing Ministerial Education themselves, that they receive no grants for robes, that they may not have access to appropriate study space.

(g)   Many respondents felt that they were not accepted as a 'proper' priest by other clergy – indeed, that they were 'second class'. Several examples of this were offered, some in considerable detail. Support from the incumbent was considered central to the LNSM's experience, and in some cases this was not forthcoming. This situation can lead to anxiety, frustration and disillusionment. While LNSMs 'muddle on', as one respondent says: 'I don't think it an adequate response merely to hope it will go away!' Some respondents thought that other members of the church needed (re)training to work effectively with LNSMs.

CHAPTER 5

Vocation and selection

5.1   The ABM Policy Paper No. 1 makes it clear that Local Non-Stipendiary Ministers are men and women locally chosen, locally trained, and locally deployed, and that the word 'local' is appropriately used of the principal source of vocation (p. 8). It goes on to say, though, that 'a call to ministry from the parish to an individual must be validated by the bishop who represents the rest of the diocese and the wider Church to which he will look for advice' (2.26). It is the function of the local church to initiate this process. 'It is a mark of Local Non-Stipendiary Ministers that they should have been invited by the local church to set out on the path towards ordination.' How that invitation comes about varies from scheme to scheme. In 1992, when there were only four schemes approved by the House of Bishops (Lincoln, Truro, Manchester and Southwark), ABM Ministry Paper No. 4, *A Review of LNSM Schemes*, identified three different models of vocation.

5.2   'LNSM schemes attempt' said that paper 'to give a real place to the idea that the Church itself is the primary recipient of vocation, and therefore that it may be by the medium of the Church that an individual receives his or her vocation to ministry. Within this general pattern, these four schemes operate with different models of calling to ministry in general (on the one hand) and to ordained ministry (on the other).' (p. 52)

5.3   The three models may be summarized briefly as follows:

(a)   A call from the Church to various individuals to form a ministry team. That team is called and formed to meet needs previously identified by the local church. Within the context of that team the parish may look, after a year or so, to see whether any member of that team is being called to ordination. There is thus a call to ministry by the Church, from which comes a personal call from God to ordained ministry discerned by the Church.

(b)   The local church considers its needs, and the qualities of potential candidates within it, and on this basis calls him or her out. The candidate will also be expected to demonstrate an inward calling to ministry.

(c)   Candidates are called to ordination by the Church, but nothing is said about an inward or 'personal' sense of call being necessary on the part of the candidate.

5.4   In practice these have often proved less distinct than they sound. In discussing the three models the Lichfield LNSM Scheme comments helpfully:

> The difficulty of analysing vocations in terms of one or other of these models, however, is that to do so may not leave much room either for varieties of personality type and subjective experience, or the different ways in which the Holy Spirit works in the concrete circumstances of individual lives and local churches. (p. 28)

5.5   It is important to be pragmatic and sensible about the varieties of ways in which vocation to ministry may emerge. However, when the call is initiated by the individual, the local church must have the opportunity to endorse that sense of vocation or not, otherwise it would be totally inappropriate for the particular candidate to be a candidate for local non-stipendiary ministry rather than non-stipendiary or stipendiary.

5.6   A small and vulnerable congregation may sometimes need diocesan help in declining the self-initiated candidacy of a forceful or domineering person. Just occasionally a candidate who is self-promoting for LNSM does get through parish and diocesan systems. References from incumbent and/or congregational colleagues usually put selectors on their guard but it is helpful if sponsoring papers are as honest as possible in these circumstances. Normally, though, such a candidate should not get as far as a selection conference.

5.7   A further important insight in the Lichfield document is this:

It must be the local church which has the determinative voice
in this process of testing vocations, on the understanding that,
where ordained LNSMs are concerned, the diocesan bishop
will make the final decision about whether a candidate should
be ordained. (p. 29)

5.8   The way in which the vocation is tested initially will vary from
scheme to scheme, but it is important to remember that prior to the
selection of the candidate, the parish will have been approved as an appropriate centre for LNSM. As the Carlisle LNSM document puts it:

There are two vocations to be tested: that of the candidate for
the priestly ministry and that of the local church for this
development in the shared ministry. (p. 145)

5.9   There is a broad range about what schemes expect in terms of
understanding and articulation of vocation. The St Edmundsbury and
Ipswich scheme says, 'Candidates should be able to speak of their sense of
vocation to ministry and mission, referring both to their own conviction
and to the extent to which others have confirmed it' and goes on, 'their
vocation should be obedient, realistic and informed.' There is a clear
expectation of personal sense of vocation here, although the document
goes on to say that it must be recognized 'that the vocation may well have
come primarily from the church community and be accepted by the candidate'.

5.10   Whether the emphasis of an LNSM scheme is on the individual or
the local church identifying a sense of call it is important that at a selection conference the candidate should be able to provide evidence to the
selectors of 'owning' that sense of vocation. This is a difficult phrase to
pin down but has something to do with showing the potential to become
what one has been invited to be.

5.11   To acknowledge fully the local in the selection conference setting
it is important to set the candidate's understanding of what he or she is
being asked to do, against the parish profile, job description and LNSM

officer's report to see if they match up, and set both against the specific diocesan submission.

5.12   The survey asked the question 'How did you come to recognise that God wanted you to be a priest?' The responses were coded according to three themes:

> Personal   (strong desire, sense of personal calling)
>
> Vicar   (encouragement from another priest)
>
> Congregation   (encouragement from local church community)

Of those who answered the question 26 mentioned a personal theme, 19 said vicar and 40 said congregation. The most significant theme for 30 respondents was personal, while congregation was most significant for 27, and vicar for 5.

5.13   Some responses are shown here:

Personal: 'A calling from God spanning over twenty years during which time I was turned away from ministry on academic grounds. So I thank God for his continued calling of me, for the path given to me and that he does not leave all his selection in the hands of mere mortals.'

'Clear call from God – like a cockerel calling across a farmyard.'

'I asked Him in prayer and then I put it into His hands. It is a similar pattern to motherhood, the waiting, the pain, sleepless nights where you question yourself, bonding, nourishing and the joy.'

Personal, vicar
and congregation: 'I felt called by God and decided not to say anything for a week. During that week my incumbent, husband and a church reader shared their thoughts that I should consider ministry.'

Personal and congregation:	'The initial idea came from outside – from our congregation – when our team was called into being. Over the years a gradual inner conviction grew that this was what God wanted for me.'
Personal and vicar:	'I had carefully planned what I was going to do when I retired. However, when my vicar suggested that I be ordained, it immediately seemed to me that that was what God wanted me to do, and that the other activities which I had planned were not His will for me.'
Congregation:	'I was called by 46 people (100 per cent) in two PCCs to assist in supplying their spiritual needs.'
Personal and congregation:	'The congregation requested me to take on this role. After some years of consideration I felt I could usefully serve in this way.'
	'Call from the local congregation and growing personal awareness of a calling.'

5.14   The Norwich LNSM Scheme offers these helpful notes for examining chaplains:

Diocese of Norwich NSM Training Scheme

NOTES ON LNSM CANDIDATES FOR EXAMINING CHAPLAINS

For LNSM candidates you will need to answer the usual questions, as for other candidates, but bearing in mind the differences between LNSM and other forms of ministry. This means:-

1.	*The Vocation* to LNSM may come essentially from the calling out of the Local Church which the candidate has made his/her own: Is there evidence both of his community call and of a personal vocation?

2.	*Spirituality:* LNSM requires a spiritual stability (in a Benedictine sense) which is different from the kind of flexibility required of those whose ministry is expected to be mobile – is this kind of stability a gift of which there is evidence?

3.	*Leadership and Collaboration:* We are selecting a candidate for his/her own particular local community: what understanding of this localness is there?

4.	*Quality of mind:* For LNSM the training in ministerial preparation and the intellectual demands of ministry are different than for other forms of ordained ministry.

Both the training and the subsequent ministry are fully shared in a way which makes individual achievement and progress harder to monitor apart from growth of the whole collaborative scene in the parish/benefice.

Every stage of ministry is carried out under the close view of the Local Ministry Team, and the whole local church, in a way which makes different personal demands on the student.

5.15   At a selection conference the wider church, with strong local representation, offers criteria accepted by the whole church, against which the call may be tested. It seeks to discern in a candidate that which has been identified locally, a vocation to serve and a vocation to stay, recognizing that in Local Non-Stipendiary Ministry the vocation of the individual should not be separate from the vision of the parish.

5.16   The evidence from studying the texts of diocesan LNSM schemes, reinforced by visits to schemes, confirms that the identification of potential LNSMs and the selection of them is a rigorous process. In fact there are generally two distinct elements of identification of the suitability of the parish or locality as a context for local ministry followed by the selection of a candidate or team. There are a variety of approaches in the diocesan schemes but generally the local candidate for ordination may only be put forward either where there is already an established ministry team, or where there is strong evidence of shared or collaborative ministry, or evidence of the potential for it. We affirm the importance of the selection of the parish or locality and **recommend that this should be the responsibility of the LNSM officer, or person or group of persons appointed by the bishop for this purpose.**

5.17   **We recommend that clear documentation about the parish or locality should be sent with papers relating to a candidate's selection conference.**

5.18   At present a candidate may be sponsored to a Bishop's Conference either before entering training or after the first year of training, according to the rule of a diocesan scheme. We are content to commend both practices but in the latter case especially, particular care will need to be given to the non-recommended candidate. LNSM officers will need to be aware of the ABM guidelines relating to the care of candidates published in 1997 (Ministry Paper No. 16). In the context of a non-recommendation, the parish or locality can feel a great sense of non-recommendation or rejection itself. Something which a parish or locality has nurtured and requested, i.e. the vocation and ordination of one of its members, has been denied by the wider church. Again, it should be part of the role of the LNSM officer to respond to these feelings.

5.19   Dioceses with approved LNSM schemes may send candidates to national selection conferences, or hold a selection conference locally with an ABM Selection Secretary and an external bishop's selector taking part. In the case of conferences held locally ABM guidelines must be followed, and until 1997 local conferences were almost identical to national conferences in structure and context, although they generally took place over a weekend rather than midweek.

5.20   The disadvantage felt by some to be inherent in the attendance of LNSM candidates at a national selection conference is that such a conference is not primarily set up to deal with the particularities of LNSM. Selectors are not necessarily familiar with LNSM and may therefore find it hard to come to grips with the assessment of LNSM candidates. This can to some extent be overcome by the ABM Selection Secretary's wider experience. It has tended to be felt in the past that LNSM candidates do not fare so well at a national conference, although the feeling one picks up around the LNSM schemes is that this has improved and that schemes are feeling more confident about using national conferences. A positive advantage of attendance at a national selection conference is that it gives the selection process a higher credibility, especially among clergy.

5.21   The disadvantage of diocesan selection conferences are that they may be seen as a 'soft option', weighted heavily in favour of the candidate. This is often a complaint of clergy who are hostile to LNSM, and so the 'back door' suspicion tends to be reinforced by this method of selection. The other main disadvantage is that it can be difficult in a diocese to muster the required number of candidates for this one occasion in the year, with some candidates being kept hanging around for a long time after their nomination in the parish, and others just missing the one annual selection conference.

5.22   Throughout the development of LNSM some dioceses have usually sent candidates to national selection conferences while others have usually organized conferences locally. Some dioceses use national selection when they have only a few candidates while they organize local conferences when they have sufficient candidates. We now also have experience of two neighbouring dioceses with similar schemes sharing a local conference on a regular basis, and there are examples of three dioceses sharing a conference. We want to affirm the possibility of dioceses sending candidates to national or local selection and to commend the practice of dioceses sharing conferences where practical, particularly on a regional basis.

5.23   One further reflection in this general area is the effect on groups of candidates of going to selection conferences together and then entering training together. This happens in dioceses which mount their own selection conferences. The experience (unique to LNSM, because other ordinands come together in training groups from a number of different selection conferences) has a most interesting effect, which seems to persist throughout and even beyond training. The group bonds rapidly at the selection conference, with a bonding which is, of course, strongly reinforced when those recommended for training (the survivors) begin the course. This bonding is of course of great initial value educationally because a substantial degree of trust in the group has already been established. But there is a question about it too. Is the degree of bonding altogether healthy, or does it result in a subconscious collusion and lack of challenge within the group? The repercussions of the 'lifeboat' experience are powerful and not necessarily all positive. This might argue for exploration of something like regional selection conferences.

5.24   In 1995 a Working Party report was published, *A Review of Selection Procedures in the Church of England* (ABM Policy Paper No. 6). The Working Party recommended an overhaul of selection procedures, including the introduction of two cognitive tests (one of verbal organization, the other of deductive reasoning), the revision of group and written exercises, and a significant change in the role of the Conference Secretary. After a year of training, induction and preparation the new procedures were introduced to national selection conferences in January 1997.

5.25   The Selection Procedures Working Party's second recommendation was that 'LNSM should be the subject of a separate review set up within the next two years', and its proposals did not apply to selection conferences held locally. Thus, during 1997 and 1998 LNSM candidates coming to national selection conferences are being assessed under the new procedures, while those attending local conferences are being assessed under the old procedure.

5.26   We have consulted widely with LNSM officers, course principals and the Recruitment and Selection Committee of ABM. While we are happy with the possibility of national or local selection, we are clear that the procedures should follow the same pattern. This is to maintain the integrity of LNSM selection for the sake of those offering for that form of ministry and also to help reassure those who remain opposed to, or suspicious of it.

5.27   LNSM officers will need to be trained in the new procedures and **we recommend that this shall be the responsibility of the Senior Selection Secretary and LNSM Coordinator of ABM.**

5.28   In the same way that the cognitive tests were administered to ordinands in training to establish the usefulness and validity of the tests, **we recommend that volunteers training on LNSM schemes should undergo the tests to establish the suitability of the tests for use in LNSM selection.**

5.29   **We recommend that the new selection procedures should be applied to Bishops' Selection Conferences held locally from the beginning of 1999.**

5.30   The role of the diocesan director of ordinands in the preparation of LNSM candidates for selection conferences varies from one LNSM scheme to another. To ensure consistency of information provided about all candidates offering for training for ordination **we recommend that sponsoring papers approved by the House of Bishops and contained in ABM Policy Paper No. 6 (pp.70ff.) should be the papers used in the sponsoring of a candidate and offered to bishops' selectors.** Where a DDO has no direct responsibility for

LNSM candidates LNSM officers will need to be familiar with the use of sponsoring papers. Generally though we would expect LNSM sponsorship to be integrated with diocesan policy about sponsorship of candidates for other categories of ministry. **We recommend that DDOs meet with and interview LNSM candidates and maintain a close relationship with LNSM officers.**

5.31   ABM Policy Paper No. 1 comments somewhat wryly (p. 33), 'If the church is serious about the "local" character of LNSM it should neither find these limitations (i.e. of licence) surprising, nor the whole question of transfer to another location as fraught with difficulty.' Clearly in an ideal world those sponsored, recommended for training and ordained as LNSMs would remain so, and, it must be said, in most cases they do when a transfer becomes necessary. The transfer envisaged is usually one of three kinds: transfer to another category of ministry, transfer as an LNSM to another area within the diocese, or transfer to a different diocese.

5.32   The report *A Review of Selection Procedures in the Church of England* (ABM Policy Paper No. 6) recommended that in order to clarify the task of selection in dioceses and centrally, new categories for sponsorship should be introduced (p. 24).

These are:

> Ordained Ministry (LNSM)
> Ordained Ministry (Permanent NSM)
> Ordained Ministry (SM and NSM)
> Accredited Lay Ministry (SM and NSM)
> Accredited Lay Ministry (Permanent NSM)

5.33   These categories of sponsorship have been effective since 1 January 1997. The reorganization of categories recognizes that there will be candidates for whom it will be appropriate to move between stipendiary and non-stipendiary posts during the course of ministry and the revised category facilitates this. The distinct category Ordained

Ministry (LNSM) emphasizes the fact that LNSM is a distinct vocation to 'stickability' rather than deployment as a priest.

5.34   Generally we are impressed by the care with which the diocese and candidate arrive at the appropriate form of sponsorship. The requests for transfer are thus few. However, in the case of transfer from LNSM to NSM or SM after selection but before ordination, the sponsoring bishop should refer candidates to the Recruitment and Selection Committee of ABM. The committee will advise the bishop about the desirability of transfer and about suitable training.

5.35   It seems clear to us that when a LNSM moves, either within the diocese or outside, he or she ceases to be local. Obviously he or she remains a priest, but there must be a strong possibility that such ministers who move from place to place may not receive the Bishop's Licence to exercise ordained ministry. This needs to be made clear at the time of sponsorship, and in our experience, usually is. We concur with Policy Paper No. 1 (cf. 6.7–6.13) that when a move is within a diocese there will have to be consideration of the minister's own record and then of his or her stability in the new location, of the LNSM status of a new parish and of its preparedness to receive the minister as a Local Non-Stipendiary. Such consideration will take time. Evidence will be required of collaborative ministry in the new parish. In the case of a move to another diocese where there may be a different kind of LNSM scheme or no scheme at all, advice should be sought from the Recruitment and Selection Committee of ABM about a change of category of ordained ministry.

CHAPTER 6

Training and finance

Models of training

6.1   Among the schemes so far accredited by the House of Bishops and moderated by ABM there is considerable diversity in the method, style, context and content of training. In 1992 a Working Party of the Initial Ministerial Education Committee produced the report *A Review of LNSM Schemes: Developments of Models of Ministry and Training in Recent Diocesan Proposals for LNSM* (ABM Ministry Paper No. 4). The report examined the four schemes for LNSM which had so far been accredited: Lincoln, Manchester, Truro and Southwark. Three emerging models were identified:

Model A: an integrated approach to training lay and ordained members for Local Ministry Teams;

Model B: the training of ordinands for LNSM within local groups which are not Local Ministry Teams;

Model C: the training only of ordinands for LNSM, where the training takes place in diocesan groups with other ordinands for LNSM.

6.2   The present picture, with fourteen schemes for LNSM so far accredited and others in the course of preparation, is more complex. The diversity in training provision reflects a number of factors. These include:

the diocesan approach to local ministry teams (formal or organic);

diocesan and regional training resources;

the nature of the diocese (urban, rural);

diocesan organization of training (e.g. lay training, training for Readers).

Decisions about appropriate patterns of training for LNSM must take into account such factors and must also – most important of all – achieve a balance in the *contexts* of training which will

(a)   promote the development of collaborative ministry in the parish;

(b)   support the training of the local ministry team;

(c)   ensure that the LNSMs receive proper ministerial formation and ordination training.

What we see in the present diversity among schemes is an exploration of ways in which this balance may best be achieved.

6.3   Training for LNSM will have two primary contexts. The first is the parish. Here the LNSM will train alongside members of a team or group. It is here that collaborative working will grow. Theology and praxis go hand in hand in this local setting as the group develops and learns together. The second context is the peer group of LNSMs in the wider context of the diocese. Here, other aspects of training, including some aspects of ministerial formation and rigorous and in-depth theological study, will be undertaken. In some LNSM schemes this will primarily be provided internally, in others it will be achieved mainly through work with a regional part-time course; in others by a mixture of the two.

6.4   Some schemes (e.g. Manchester and Southwark) provide the whole course of LNSM training themselves; others (e.g. Gloucester and Norwich) provide parts of the training themselves and 'buy into nearby part-time courses or colleges for some training; others (e.g. Carlisle) utilize a part-time course for the whole of their training programme; others (e.g. Lichfield) provide the training primarily through an integrated diocesan programme for lay training, Reader training and LNSM training. Each of these approaches (and they represent points on a broad spectrum of approaches to LNSM training) has its advantages and disadvantages.

6.5   It is at this stage in the development of LNSM impossible, we believe, to make hard and fast statements about which approach to training is to be preferred. The variations between dioceses are such that a reasonable flexibility in the range of schemes seems to us to be not only desirable but essential, if LNSM is to flourish in a variety of settings. After receiving a large amount of written and verbal evidence, the Working Party has not found it either possible or desirable to say that any one of the current range of LNSM training schemes, or even one end of the spectrum, is clearly to be preferred to any other.

6.6   It would appear, and the early evidence from the House of Bishops' Inspections of Schemes bears this out, that in those schemes where there is a particular bias towards the parish context of the training, there tend to be difficulties in achieving priestly formation. Conversely, in those schemes where a larger proportion of the training is in the LNSM peer group, there may be deficiencies in the development of the local team. Thus the key task in the design of schemes and, in particular, in the design of LNSM training is the achieving of a balance of elements, so as to foster both the local growth in collaborative ministry and to ensure the clear and unequivocal formation of LNSMs for their ordained ministry.

We recommend that at present there continues to be diversity (appropriate to local diocesan needs and priorities) in the range and type of training provision accredited by ABM and the House of Bishops, and that careful attention is given to the balance of training elements, so as to promote the training and growth of the local ministry team and to ensure the proper ministerial formation of LNSM candidates.

6.7   We have identified a number of specific areas of good practice which should be part of any course of training accredited for LNSM and we have seen during our consultations that there are key factors which must be taken into account in the provision of training for LNSM.

Method

6.8 LNSM is at its heart collaborative. Therefore the styles and methods of teaching and learning must be pervaded by a collaboration that is wholehearted and which does not merely pay lip service to the notion. It will set standards and enable individuals and groups to identify their own potential. At all points it will encourage and challenge individuals to be clear about their own faith and vocation but at the same time always to see that faith and vocation in the corporate context. We do not expect to hear LNSMs talk about 'my ministry'.

6.9 Modern understanding of adult learning shows that it is most effective when grounded in experience. The previous experience, knowledge and skills of the learner are not only taken seriously but form the starting point in learning. This experiential or transformative learning is by nature collaborative, since the group and its leader work together to carry learning forward. We have included in this report a paper on 'Transformative Education' by David Leslie, of the Liverpool LNSM Scheme, since we believe this method to be of such fundamental importance in LNSM training (see Appendix 5 on p. 122).

6.10 It will be clear from this, and from what has been said in a previous chapter about collaboration, that the experiential or transformative educational method should be central to the style of LNSM training. Collaboration is learned by collaborating. This does not mean that LNSM training will be lacking in input. On the contrary, it is through this method that very substantial and profound theological enquiry and learning will take place. It does rely, however, upon skilled teaching from tutors who are widely knowledgeable and competent in theological education and possess expert knowledge in various theological disciplines. It relies also upon the establishment of a sound peer group or groups for training, since it requires significant time in the group together for ideas to be explored and developed and connections made between different areas of knowledge.

6.11 Most LNSMs will have at least two important peer groups during their training. The first, and basic unit, is the local ministry team, in which much group learning, pastoral development and collaborative formation will take place. The second is the peer group of LNSM ordinands in the diocese, who will come together for training for a larger or smaller number of sessions, depending on the diocesan scheme. If there is a training relationship with a part-time course there will be further peer groups.

6.12   We believe it to be important for the success of LNSM training that LNSMs are not expected to relate to too many peer groups, but that there is some real continuity over time in the groups within which the LNSM is learning. If the number of such groups is too many, or if their membership changes continually, then the important continuities of learning (the 'spiral' pattern) are likely to be lost. The limiting of the number of learning groups of which a LNSM should be a member during training is a necessary balance and check in the use of the 'portfolio' method which is in vogue today. In the 'portfolio' method the present skills and knowledge of the individual are analysed against a list of competencies which the person needs to acquire during training. This analysis is then used to determine the person's path through training, with selections being made according to the competencies needing to be acquired. We are in no doubt that this method has educational value and that it is a helpful means of assessing a range of training needs. We are clear, however, that it is an approach which is fundamentally individualistic and must, therefore, be used with care in ministerial formation. We believe this to be true for all ministerial formation, but especially for LNSM training. 'Portfolio' can be used to good effect in particular aspects of ministerial training (liturgical training being an excellent example), but is of less value where collaborative and group skills are of paramount importance.

Context

6.13   A careful balancing of the contexts of training is critical for LNSM. The training in some schemes takes place largely within the parish; in other schemes much of the training will take place elsewhere, with parts or aspects of the training being based in the parish. Whatever the overall balance it is crucial that the two are genuinely complementary and that the complementarity is explicit.

6.14 We have come across instances where the style and ethos of the parish-based training are significantly at odds with the style and ethos of the training taking place elsewhere. Such divergence can be a danger where there is a large element in the training of work done with one of the regional part-time courses, and especially where the numbers of LNSMs in training are very small. This is clearly damaging to the ministerial formation of individual LNSMs and it fundamentally undermines the whole process of the training of LNSM teams. Hence the damage done if the balance is wrong is not confined to the individual LNSM: it can affect the whole life and development of the parish.

6.15 LNSMs cannot learn to be collaborative priests if they are faced throughout their training by a fundamental dichotomy of view – on the one hand the collaborative ethos of the local ministry team, and on the other an implicitly or explicitly individualistic ethos generated by an institution which is training candidates for stipendiary and non-stipendiary ministry and is not concerned primarily with the distinctively collaborative ethos of LNSM. We put this quite bluntly, not from any lack of appreciation of the quality and integrity of colleges and courses, but because our consultations have revealed widespread disquiet on this issue.

6.16 The pursuit of joint training is valuable if it promotes awareness of diversity in ministry and fosters a spirit of mutual respect and affirmation. We believe that the LNSM schemes already established have much to offer the colleges and courses, and we would encourage all concerned to find ways of sharing resources and expertise. LNSM schemes need to take their full part in the development of regional resources in theological education, in line with established ABM policy as expressed in the final report of the ABM Steering Group (ABM Ministry Paper No. 12) and updated in the Chief Secretary's report *Issues in Theological Education and Training* (ABM Ministry Paper No. 15). The membership of the annual National Consultation for LNSM Schemes demonstrates the extraordinarily rich resource of experience, theological ability and collaborative expertise of those who are staffing LNSM schemes.

6.17   There are advantages to be gained from LNSM ordinands working with ordinands for stipendiary and non-stipendiary ministry during training. Such contact broadens the horizons of all concerned. We have discovered from our consultations that there are still large numbers of ordinands in training for stipendiary and non-stipendiary ministry, and many clergy recently ordained, who appear to have had inadequate preparation for collaborative styles of ministry and who are insufficiently informed about LNSM. Joint opportunities in training can go a long way towards breaking down barriers of ignorance and hostility.

6.18   However, this cannot happen unless the joint training is training that will genuinely promote mutual understanding. Nor can it happen unless the reasons for coming together for particular pieces of training have been clearly identified. Where there is to be joint training the educational aims, objectives and methods must be carefully examined. Whilst joint training has some clear advantages, not least in the efficient use of resources, it must be undertaken for reasons that are clearly thought through, not simply because in a vague way it is believed to be good to bring people together or to be a better use of resources (important though that is). In its work with dioceses and with courses and colleges on proposals for joint training, the Education Validation Sub-Committee of ABM must ensure that there has been sufficient examination of the educational purpose of joint training. We believe it to be crucial to LNSM training that any proposed joint training should be fully and explicitly justified on educational grounds rather than taking the starting-point to be the justification of separate training. **We recommend that for any joint training there is a clear educational rationale which does full justice to the requirements and ethos of LNSM training.**

Educational accessibility

6.19   Most part-time courses and all theological colleges now have some form of external validation with an institution of higher education. Where LNSM schemes have a relationship with courses and colleges this raises its own important questions. On the one hand it has the positive advantage that ordinands and lay people within LNSM training may be able to come within the validation scheme and so receive external credit for study. At the same time the requirements of validated training may place constraints upon flexible patterns of training. A number of officers working in the field of LNSM training, including those who have broad experience in theological education, have expressed anxiety that joint work with colleges and courses may be seriously and inappropriately constrained by the requirements of external validation arrangements.

6.20   We can illustrate this with the example of a regional course which has an intake of students of whom over 90 per cent are graduates. The course's validation agreement, not surprisingly, pitches all its validated modules at a level no lower than third year undergraduate equivalent. Now if such a course is providing part of the training for a LNSM scheme, there will need to be very careful negotiation about the level, style, content and assessment of work, if the needs of a more diverse LNSM group are to be catered for. We need to be careful that, at the same time as courses are establishing and developing their relationships with institutions of higher education, LNSM schemes are able to develop and to sustain their distinctive training ethos and their educational accessibility.

Physical accessibility of training

6.21   Whilst there are unlikely to be problems with access in the parish-based components of LNSM training, there are important issues in relation to central components of the training. For training which is being provided in the diocese or on a course it will be important to ensure that there is easy access by road, rail and other public transport. In large rural dioceses as well as in urban settings, transport may well be an issue. If LNSM is truly to be a ministry which is indigenous and one which will foster the ministries of a wide spectrum of people, then attention to such issues is important for future development. Present national profiles of LNSMs show a rather narrow socio-economic grouping, but the urban schemes, such as Manchester, Liverpool and Southwark, are strongly committed to developing indigenous inner-urban ministries and are training people of very diverse backgrounds.

Staffing of LNSM schemes

6.22   Training for LNSM is a complex operation, requiring a high level of experience and theological and educational skill. We have seen evidence of a high level of competence, skill and creativity among the staffs of the LNSM schemes. We note, though, that very often principals and key staff members are seriously over-stretched.   In most schemes the core staff is too small and there is over-reliance on the goodwill of parish clergy and others to undertake teaching and pastoral support. This under-resourcing will in the long run undermine the development of LNSM and must be addressed realistically.

6.23   We are aware that in some cases teachers used by LNSM schemes for elements of training, (sometimes those provided at local level, but sometimes also those provided centrally or even on courses) may not have adequate skills in adult education. Bearing in mind the importance of the experiential or transformative method for achieving training for collaborative ministry, we believe it is essential that all involved in LNSM training (whether at local or central levels) are adequately experienced and equipped. Proven experience and knowledge of the principles and methods of modern adult education must be required of all who teach LNSM candidates. **We recommend that no one should tutor on LNSM schemes or teach LNSM candidates unless they are properly equipped in adult education skills or enabled to acquire such skills.**

Training facilities

6.24   It is essential that dioceses with LNSM schemes take seriously the responsibility to provide a good training base for central aspects of the training. There should be well-equipped, comfortable and accessible rooms, with sufficient capacity to enable collaborative work with other groups in training, e.g. Readers, to take place.

6.25   There is some evidence that LNSM schemes are significantly under-resourced by their dioceses. We believe that dioceses with LNSM schemes must recognize their financial obligations. LNSM and the wider developments of collaborative ministry are frequently referred to in diocesan vision and strategy documents as high priorities, yet the practical resourcing of schemes does not always appear to match the rhetoric.

6.26   There is evidence too that LNSM candidates do not have sufficiently good access to books and other learning resources. All too often candidates are prevented from following up topics and lines of research because they do not have the resources to do so. LNSM candidates must have access to good library facilities, if possible in the same place as the central training base(s). They should also receive book grants on a par with all other ordinands.

Biblical and doctrinal study

6.27   In LNSM training the study of the Bible and of Christian doctrine, together with the other theological disciplines, is likely to be done in part in the parish context and in part elsewhere. The integration of learning in the various contexts is of key importance. It is important too that whatever the context of particular learning there should be theological and intellectual rigour and consistency. (This need not and must not compromise educational accessibility.) LNSMs are ordained into the whole catholic Church and they require theological competence and doctrinal understanding which are consonant with the exercise of priesthood. For LNSMs to be poorly equipped in this regard makes them vulnerable in their ministry and weakens the corporate and collaborative ministry of which they are part. **We recommend that the Education Validation Sub-Committee ensures that all LNSM schemes make adequate provision for training in doctrinal and biblical studies.**

Spirituality in LNSM training

6.28   We believe that the particular and long-term demands of LNSM require that special attention is paid to spiritual formation. The ministry of a LNSM will need to be sustained, refreshed and renewed over long periods in a single locality. This places great demands upon the spirituality of the LNSM, particularly since he or she will need to continue to discover and to share fresh and deepening insights with others in the parish: in other words the health and vitality of the LNSM's spirituality will fundamentally affect the health and vitality of the corporate whole and vice versa.

6.29   For this reason we believe that the element of spirituality in LNSM training must be given close and rigorous attention, ensuring that those in training have every opportunity to explore and to deepen their own spirituality, to experience varieties of spiritual tradition and above all to be nurtured in these ancient and deep models of corporate spirituality which can be found, for example, in the Benedictine and the Anglican traditions. **We recommend that LNSM training, for ordinands and for the whole team, should pay special attention to spiritual nurture.**

Preaching

6.30   LNSM schemes have not all assumed that LNSMs would preach regularly. Some have taken the view that, in the context of collaborative ministry and the recognition of differing gifts and skills, it should be possible for people to exercise an ordained ministry which does not regularly involve preaching or teaching. Two comments must be made on this. The first is that such a view is at odds with the Ordinal, and hence with the fundamental understanding in the Church of England about what a priest is and does. Even allowing for the proper differentiation of gifts and ministries within the collaborative context, it is inescapably the case that a priest should have some measure of ability to expound the faith in preaching and in teaching, even though that function may not be among the principal tasks undertaken by a particular individual. The second important point is that we know that LNSMs are preaching regularly. Our survey showed that nearly a third of LNSMs preach once or twice a month at a Sunday service in their benefice, and a further 27 per cent preach three or four times a month at a Sunday service. A few preach even more.

So it is clear that in actual fact LNSMs are expected to preach frequently, whatever the main pastoral emphasis of their ministry. In the light of the Ordinal and in the light of our research into actual practice, the importance of training in preaching (in formal and less formal settings) and generally in communication skills is clear.

We recommend that the Education Validation Sub-Committee ensures that all LNSM schemes make adequate provision for training in preaching and communication and liturgy.

Liturgical training

6.31 As in the case of preaching, the Ordinal and the experience of LNSM in practice make it clear that a thorough training in liturgical understanding and skills is necessary. This can best be achieved through a combination of training shared by LNSM ordinands and work at local level with the incumbent and other appropriate people. A clear scheme of study and practice should be established so as to enable the LNSM to acquire competence in the full range of services, including a basic competence with the occasional offices, even if their conduct of some of these will be rare.

6.32 Liturgical training should include a range of experience of different styles and contexts of worship beyond the home parish. This can be achieved through placements and also through regular occasional visits to other parishes throughout the training period, with opportunity for analyses and reflection on the experience.

6.33 Liturgical training will be spread over the full period of training, and it is vital that a journal/portfolio is kept and regularly updated, so that learning can be measured both by the candidate and by those responsible for the training.

Placements

6.34   These are an essential ingredient of LNSM training. LNSMs are ordained with a specific locality as the focus for their ministry. Many of them are long-established in their parish. Our survey showed that out of sixty-five respondents none had lived in their benefice for less than five years; eleven had lived there between five and ten years; and thirty-six had lived there for more than ten years. The long experience of LNSMs in their own locality is an important strength. Yet as priests and deacons of the whole Church they must also have an awareness of its differing traditions. Some of this wider awareness will come from their theological study, but some must come too from a living experience of different contexts. To learn more of the vocation of the people of God in their own locality they need to have some experience of the life of the people of God in other places.

6.35   Consideration should also be given to appropriate secular placements and experience during the course of training. As a means of deepening the candidate's understanding of the Church in society they are an invaluable reflective tool, and help too to broaden the training context. It is important that LNSM training should not lie wholly within the gathered church, and additional elements, such as visits of observation to secular agencies and institutions and community projects in the candidate's own localities are of great value.

6.36   The placement, carefully integrated into the whole programme of training, thus makes an important contribution to the ministerial formation of LNSM candidates. **We recommend that all LNSM candidates undertake a substantial placement in another parish during their training.**

Integrating training undertaken in different contexts

6.37   LNSM training will always have discrete components. It is rooted in the parish, and especially in the local team, however that is constituted. But it will also contain elements which are undertaken elsewhere by those members of the team who are being prepared for ordination. This may happen in a diocesan-wide LNSM training group or in the context of a course or in the context of a theological college. The 'mixed economy' of training is characteristic of LNSM. It can be a strength and it can also be a weakness.

6.38   We have considered carefully the relationship between discrete components of training, and the effects upon LNSM ordinands and upon the lay teams with whom they are training and working in the parish. One of the dangers of the LNSM ordinand going away from the parish for training is that this can undermine the collaborative growth of the whole team and send out wrong signals of status and worth to laypeople. Similarly, the LNSM can become theologically distanced from the Local Ministry Team and could become personally isolated by the training undertaken elsewhere. We believe, therefore, that there must be a careful examination of the ways in which the LNSM can bring back to the team the theology, the skills and the experience gained elsewhere, and that this must be clearly apparent in the design of LNSM training. So if, for instance, LNSMs in a particular diocese attend sessions on the atonement at the nearest theological college, the educational design must include provision for the LNSMs to share with their parish team what they have learnt. Similarly, where (as in schemes such as Manchester and Southwark) the LNSMs meet weekly for diocesan-wide training, the educational design must make explicit the ways in which aspects of the course content will be shared in the collaborative setting in the parish.

Length of training before ordination

6.39   Accredited schemes for LNSM have, in general a pattern of a three year training, done on a part-time basis. There are instances where the training is clearly understood to be for a four-year period, extending beyond ordination to the diaconate. The majority of schemes, however, have a three year training, with ordination to the diaconate at the end of that time, followed by ordination to the priesthood a year later.

6.40   It has been put to us that ordination to the diaconate after two years in training, with a further year or two years in training, is desirable for LNSM. The main argument in favour of this suggests that it is better for LNSMs to experience the start of their ordained ministry, and thus their change in role in the parish, whilst still within the support structure of the training course. The experience of most schemes leads us to believe that this is neither necessary nor desirable. We do not think it desirable that parishes which have nominated LNSMs should be placed in the confusing situation of having a LNSM already ordained but still firmly within the context of initial ministerial training. To ordain LNSMs whilst they are still considered to be undergoing initial ministerial education also causes unnecessary confusion among other clergy. We believe that a full three years of ministerial formation is necessary before a recommendation about ordination can be made with confidence to the diocesan bishop. **We recommend that candidates for LNSM should undergo three years of training prior to ordination.**

Post-Ordination Training and Continuing Ministerial Education

6.41   For the good of the whole ministry of the Church of England we believe it essential that all those in their first three years of ordained ministry experience through their post-ordination training a diversity of models of ministry. Dioceses which have had LNSM schemes in existence for a number of years have given us evidence of very mixed experiences in Post-Ordination Training (POT). Where POT brings together clergy who are SM, NSM, and LNSM there are reports of hostility and misunderstanding, particularly in the early stages of joint training. We find it disturbing that there should be frequent reports of hostility towards LNSMs from newly ordained stipendiary clergy, often based upon misconceptions about the nature of LNSM and dismissive attitudes towards LNSM training or part-time training in general. However, comments from LNSMs and diocesan training officers about the improving of mutual understanding during the period of POT underlines the importance of joint training.

6.42   Some dioceses have already established good practice in POT. In Manchester, for example, a clear policy decision was taken that virtually all POT should be in mixed groups of SM, NSM and LNSM. The local tutor groups which meet at six-weekly intervals in the evenings are all mixed, and the residential sessions are held at weekends. It is clear, however, that in a number of dioceses LNSM POT is not integrated into the whole scheme, nor do LNSMs fall firmly within mainstream CME. A few LNSMs have spoken of being unable to afford to attend CME sessions because they did not have the same financial support for CME as other clergy in the diocese. Timing of sessions was also an issue for many, with POT and CME sessions being held exclusively in the daytime on weekdays, thus effectively excluding LNSMs and NSMs.

6.43   It appears that where provision for LNSMs is less than adequate there may often also be inadequate provision for NSMs. **We recommend that all dioceses with LNSM schemes should organize their POT in such a way as to ensure the full integration of LNSMs with stipendiary and non-stipendiary clergy so as to foster mutual understanding.**

We recommend that dioceses ensure the establishment of fully integrated programmes for continuing ministerial education, with parity of financial support for all clergy and a range of daytime, evening and weekend opportunities.

Support for partners and families

6.44   Some schemes have paid attention to support for partners and families, and we note that the Norwich scheme, in particular, has looked carefully at the particular pressures of LNSMs on families. LNSMs undergo a change in role from lay to ordained within their home church and community, and we are aware that this can bring pressures and misunderstandings.

We recommend that all schemes should ensure that there is proper care for the families of LNSM candidates, and should

also ensure that they are given opportunities to reflect upon the change of role and the altered expectations that may result from this.

Finance

6.45   ABM Policy Paper No. 1 looked carefully at the financing of LNSM schemes, and commended the practice by which the financing of candidates to train for LNSM is shared both by central funds and by the diocese. Such shared financial responsibility helped stress the element of catholicity in schemes for LNSM. The offer of some help from central funds also provides an incentive to the submission of LNSM schemes to the House of Bishops for approval and thereby enables a high standard to be maintained. The grant from central funds is, at present, only available to schemes approved by the House of Bishops, which ensures through ABM that selection procedures are of a high standard and are comparable from diocese to diocese.

6.46   The system proposed by Policy Paper No. 1 and subsequently adopted was one by which a block grant from central funds was made to each diocesan scheme, towards part of the salary for the principal of each scheme. Until now, the proportion of the principal's salary to be met from central funds has been determined by the Finance Committee of ABM in the light of the proportion of the principal's duties that relate to the training of candidates for LNSM.

6.47   This contribution has been appreciated by dioceses with LNSM schemes but there are disadvantages to it. These disadvantages were identified in a paper to us from the Finance Committee of ABM and are as follows:

(a)   A clumsy division operates between schemes with substantial numbers of non-ordinands (which receive a grant representing half the national maximum average of an incumbent's stipend), and schemes primarily concerned with the training of ordinands (which receive a grant for a full stipend).

(b)   The level of grant bears no relationship to the number of candidates.

(c)   Encouragement is not given for schemes to make full use of existing resources for training available to dioceses.

Regarding (c) the resources would need to be shown to be appropriate for LNSM training.

We are grateful to the Finance Committee of ABM for looking at the whole matter of financing LNSM schemes and wish to recommend a proposal put to us by that committee. It is a proposal which has the broad support of existing LNSM schemes.

6.48   **We recommend that a basic grant of £6,000 per annum is paid to a diocese to use at its discretion towards the scheme's cost. This should be coupled with a per capita sum per annum for each recommended ordinand. We recommend £600.** Where selection takes place after year one of training (as in, for example, the Lincoln and Liverpool models) the £600 for that year should be paid retrospectively for recommended candidates. The grant, plus per capita contribution could be used by the diocese towards a principal's stipend or other staff costs, or towards fees to be paid to existing training institutions.

6.49   **In addition we recommend that recommended candidates for LNSM should be eligible for reimbursement of travel costs (which should be modest given the local nature of training) and a book grant in line with recommended candidates for other categories of ministry.** These costs should be the responsibility of the diocese. At the time of ordination diocesan grants, in dioceses where they are made, should be available for provision of robes as they are for other categories of ministry. We believe that such a method of funding approved LNSM schemes maintains the spirit of co-operation between central funding and the diocese outlined above. It maintains an incentive to dioceses to provide schemes approved by the House of Bishops thus maintaining a high standard of selection and training.

6.50   The cost of LNSM to central funds has, naturally, risen greatly in the last four years with an increase in schemes from four to fourteen. The number of schemes could well rise to twenty or above within the next five years. It must be noted though that LNSM represents excellent value for money to central funds, as a simple comparison of the cost of training stipendiaries or NSMs will show. True the stipendiary and NSM are deployable, in theory at least, but the deliberate lack of mobility of the LNSM, what is elsewhere called 'the vocation to stickability' is reflected in the cost borne by individual diocesan schemes. However, it should be noted that at present a few enthusiasts are making LNSM training work on a shoestring. Many tutors are tutoring for free. If the Church is serious about wanting properly and appropriately trained LNSMs, the need for proper funding centrally and at diocesan level needs to be taken seriously.

Payment of staff

6.51   There are considerable discrepancies and irregularities between those working in theological colleges and courses and those working on LNSM schemes. The actual stipend/salary paid is variable. At present unless the diocese decides to top up the amount the principal is receiving, the principal is in fact being paid the salary of a college or course tutor who has no additional responsibilities. Fringe benefits such as book grants are often not provided for LNSM principals and other salaried staff on LNSM schemes although this would be done as a matter of course for college and course staffs. Broadly speaking, therefore, most principals of LNSM schemes would probably be better off in terms of the total package of salary plus other benefits if they were working as junior tutors on the staff of a college or course. If we want to see people of experience and high calibre applying for posts in LNSM schemes this will need to be addressed. Again this will involve each diocese with a scheme for LNSM realizing that this is not ministry 'on the cheap'.

Scrutiny and approval of LNSM schemes

6.52   Policy Paper No. 1 noted the need for an ABM Selection Secretary to be responsible for monitoring the exploration by dioceses of LNSM. Since 1994 a Selection Secretary has been in post with the role of 'LNSM Coordinator' written in as 25 per cent of the contract. We affirm the importance of this role and would expect dioceses considering the introduction of an LNSM scheme to be in touch with the LNSM Coordinator at an early stage. The Coordinator will be able to introduce the diocese to the growing LNSM network, and offer advice about setting up a scheme and preparing a scheme for consideration by the relevant committees of ABM.

6.53   A system has been developed whereby the LNSM Coordinator on receiving a diocesan submission for LNSM offers the scheme for scrutiny to the Recruitment and Selection Committee (to look particularly at those aspects of the scheme that relate to vocation and selection) and to the Initial Ministerial Education Committee which through its Educational Validation Sub-Committee examines the training proposals of a scheme. Since 1994 the scheme has also been scrutinized by the Ministry Development and Deployment Committee. This was in recognition that while it is one thing to set up an LNSM scheme, provision for its support and monitoring must be in place, and the care and review of candidates ordained in this category maintained. The questionnaire which the MDDC requires to be answered from the text of a submission is attached as Appendix 4.

6.54   We affirm and commend this careful scrutiny of schemes before commendation by ABM to the House of Bishops for approval since it recognizes:

(a)   That each scheme must comply with regulations and follow guidelines to ensure appropriate levels of recruitment, selection, training and monitoring.

(b)   That while various schemes may have strong similarities in method and rationale, each one will differ, if only slightly, from another, as the development is a response to the particular needs of a particular diocese.

6.55 All LNSM schemes are subject to Bishops' Inspections. The three schemes inspected so far have received positive reports. While the inspectors are concerned with the training of ordinands, it is important to recognize that schemes often train people who are not ordinands. **We recommend that Bishops' Inspection Teams of LNSM schemes should contain a member with an understanding of adult education training methods.**

CHAPTER 7

Summary of recommendations

1. We recommend the title 'ordained local minister' (2.65).

2. We recommend that all training for stipendiary and non-stipendiary clergy should include an understanding of LNSM (3.14).

3. We recommend that diocesan guidelines for Local Ministry Teams must clearly spell out the relationships with the PCC and must state clearly that it is the PCC with the incumbent which carries the legal responsibility in the parish (3.22).

4. We recommend that each diocesan submission to the House of Bishops should contain a rationale for wanting a LNSM scheme, and set it within the context of a diocesan strategy for ministry (3.24).

5. We recommend that a suffragan bishop (or, in dioceses with no suffragan, a member of the bishop's senior staff) should be an ex officio member of the governing body of a LNSM scheme (3.27).

6. We make the following recommendation in relation to appointments of incumbents in the context of LNSM:

    (a) The diocesan bishop should have unequivocal evidence of a prospective incumbent's commitment to shared ministry, and be sure that it is not merely a commitment to delegation.

    (b) The papers describing the parish should state clearly the present nature of collaboration in the parish and include information about any existing Local Ministry Team and LNSMs (either already ordained or in training).

(c) The prospective incumbent must meet any LNSMs in the benefice (ordained or in training) and the LNSMs must be given the opportunity to make their views known to the bishop before any offer is made.

(d) Where there is an established and commissioned Local Ministry Team, or one in the course of training, it must be made clear to the prospective incumbent that this is a 'given' in the parish.

(e) New appointees should undergo training in the diocese before moving to the new post, and must commit themselves to ongoing training (3.30).

7. We recommend that LNSM officers and principals have regular access to senior staff meetings (3.36).

8. We recommend that the selection of the parish or locality should be the responsibility of the LNSM officer, or person or group of persons appointed by the bishop for this purpose (5.16).

9. We recommend that clear documentation about the parish or locality should be sent with papers relating to a candidate's selection conference (5.17).

10. We recommend that the training of LNSM officers in the new selection procedures shall be the responsibility of the Senior Selection Secretary and LNSM Co-ordinator of ABM (5.27).

11. We recommend that volunteers training on LNSM schemes should undergo the cognitive tests to establish the suitability of the tests for use in LNSM selection (5.28).

12. We recommend that the new selection procedures should be applied to Bishops' Selection Conferences held locally from the beginning of 1999 (5.29).

13. We recommend that sponsoring papers contained in ABM Policy Paper No. 6 (pp. 70ff.) should be the papers used in the sponsoring of a candidate (5.30).

14.   We recommend that DDOs meet with and interview LNSM candidates and maintain a close relationship with LNSM officers (5.30).

15.   We recommend that at present there continues to be diversity (appropriate to local diocesan needs and priorities) in the range and type of training provision accredited by ABM and the House of Bishops, and that careful attention is given to the balance of training elements, so as to promote the training and growth of the local ministry team and to ensure the proper ministerial formation of LNSM candidates (6.6).

16.   We recommend that for any joint training there is a clear educational rationale which does full justice to the requirements and ethos of LNSM training (6.18).

17.   We recommend that no one should tutor on LNSM schemes or teach LNSM candidates unless they are properly equipped in adult education skills or enabled to acquire such skills (6.23).

18.   We recommend that the Education Validation Sub-Committee ensures that all LNSM schemes make adequate provision for training in doctrinal and biblical studies (6.27).

19.   We recommend that LNSM training, for ordinands and for the whole team, should pay special attention to spiritual nurture (6.29).

20.   We recommend that the Educational Validation Sub-Committee ensures that all LNSM schemes make adequate provision for training in preaching and communication, and liturgy. (6.30).

21.   We recommend that all LNSM candidates undertake a substantial placement in another parish during their training (6.36).

22.   We recommend that candidates for LNSM should undergo three years of training prior to ordination (6.40).

23.   We recommend that all dioceses with LNSM schemes should organize their POT in such a way as to ensure the full integration

of LNSMs with stipendiary and non-stipendiary clergy so as to foster mutual understanding (6.43).

24.   We recommend that dioceses ensure the establishment of fully integrated programmes for continuing ministerial education, with parity of financial support for all clergy and a range of day-time, evening and weekend opportunities (6.43).

25.   We recommend that all schemes shall ensure that there is proper care for the families of LNSM candidates, and should also ensure that they are given opportunities to reflect upon the change of role and the altered expectations that may result from this (6.44).

26.   We recommend that on receiving recognition of a scheme from the House of Bishops, a basic grant of £6000 per annum is paid to a diocese to use at its discretion towards the scheme's cost. This should be coupled with a per capita sum per annum for each rec-ommended ordinand. We recommend £600 (6.48).

27.   We recommend that recommended candidates for LNSM should be eligible for reimbursement of travel costs and a book grant in line with recommended candidates for other categories of min-istry. These costs should be the responsibility of the diocese (6.49).

28.   We recommend that Bishops' Inspection Teams of LNSM schemes should contain a member with an understanding of adult educa-tion training methods (6.55).

APPENDIX 1

Terms of reference
for the LNSM Working Party

1. To review the practice and rationale of LNSM schemes.

2. To investigate the context in which dioceses consider that it is appropriate for LNSM schemes to operate and to examine the place of schemes in diocesan pastoral/ministerial strategies.

3. To evaluate the theological basis for ordination in the context of LNSM.

4. To consider the relationship of Local Non-Stipendiary Ministry to other forms of ministry.

5. To consider the nature of collaboration within ministry teams and the exercise of oversight within them.

6. To examine the financing of LNSM and the way in which central funds contribute to it.

7. To review the present Bishops' Regulations and Guidelines in relation to LNSM schemes.

8. To consult widely with those involved in the development of ministry, especially with local strategies and local schemes in dioceses, with the relevant committees of ABM and other Boards and Councils, with our ecumenical partners, and others as appropriate.

9. To review ABM processes for providing advice to the House of Bishops about the recommendation of LNSM schemes.

10. To report to ABM and to make recommendations about future policy in relation to Local Non-Stipendiary Ministry.

APPENDIX 2

Criteria for a 'local ministry mandate'

Diocesan schemes have been generous in sharing with us examples of forms or guidelines used in assessing the suitability of a parish for local ministry and for interviewing potential candidates. Lichfield offers these helpful criteria for a local ministry mandate.

1. The local church (**as represented by the PCC**) is CLEAR about its PRIORITIES in mission, and clear about the KIND OF MINISTRY it needs to enable it to fulfil those priorities.

2. RELATIONSHIPS between Clergy and Laity are based on PART-NERSHIP, and expressed in COLLABORATIVE ways of being the Church together.

3. The **shared ministry of all baptized people** in both the ecclesial and 'secular' contexts is being **actively promoted and developed**.

4. Structures exist which model collaborative Ministry, and which enable church people to work in mutually supportive ways.

5. The practice of collaborative styles of Ministry includes the SHARING OF RESPONSIBILITY as well as the DELEGATING OF TASKS.

6. The Incumbent and PCC are CLEAR and AGREED about the desirability of a '**local leadership team**' and, if applicable, **local ordained ministry**.

7. There is a satisfactory AWARENESS about, AND OWNERSHIP of, the new development among the people of the Church.

APPENDIX 3

Questionnaire for
local non-stipendiary ministers

The questionnaire covers various aspects of your experience of ministry and includes some questions about your own background.

Your answers will be treated in strict confidence.

Where a question asks you to choose from a number of options, please put a tick in the appropriate box. Otherwise, write your answer in the space provided.

YOU AND YOUR BENEFICE

1. What is your name?

....

2. Which year were you ordained?

3. How many parishes are there in the benefice(s) where you exercise your ministry?

4. How many churches or chapels of ease are there in use in your benefice?

5. In which kind of area is your benefice located?   Inner city

Suburb

Market town

Rural area

Other (*please specify*)

....

6. Please indicate your current status in the benefice where you
    exercise your ministry

    Curate/NSM ☐

    Team vicar ☐

    Priest-in-charge ☐

    Other (*please specify*) ☐

....

BENEFICE STAFF

7. Including yourself, which 'staff' in total
    work in your benefice?

    Please give numbers in each category.

STIPENDIARY CLERGY	Male	Female
Vicars/rectors/priests-in-charge	☐	☐
Team rectors/team vicars	☐	☐
Curates	☐	☐
Deacons (not Curates)	☐	☐
Deaconesses (not Curates)	☐	☐
Licensed lay workers	☐	☐
Other (please specify)	☐	☐

....

NON-STIPENDIARY 'STAFF'	Male	Female
Non-stipendiary ministers	☐	☐
Retired clergy	☐	☐
Readers	☐	☐
Local Non-Stipendiary Minister	☐	☐
Local Ministry Team members	☐	☐

If any of these 'staff' occupy more than one role, please explain here.

....

8. In an average month, how many times do
    you have a staff meeting?

    Once ☐
    Twice ☐
    Three times ☐
    More than three times ☐

9. Are you expected to attend all staff meetings?

    Yes ☐
    No ☐

MINISTRY TEAMS

10. Which of the following teams/groups do you belong to?

    Please tick all that apply.

    Team Ministry ☐
    Group Ministry ☐
    Formal Local Ministry Team ☐
    Informal Local Ministry Team ☐

    If your Local Ministry Team meeting is the same as your staff meeting (see question 8 above), please move to question 12.

    If you are not a member of a Local Ministry Team, please move to question 17.

11. In an average month, how many times does your Local
    Ministry Team meet? ☐

12. How many years has your Local Ministry Team been in
    existence? ☐

13. Does your role differ from that of other
    members of the Team?

    Yes, quite a lot ☐
    Yes, somewhat ☐
    No ☐

    If your answer is 'no', please move to question 15.

14. In what way does your role differ from that of other members of the Team?

....

....

....

15. Do you think other members of the Team regard you as having a special role in the Team?

Yes, quite a lot ☐

Yes, somewhat ☐

No ☐

If your answer is 'no', please move to question 17.

16. In what way do other members of the Team regard you as having a special role in the Team?

....

....

....

YOUR PRIESTLY MINISTRY

17. How did you come to recognize that God wanted you to be a priest?

....

....

....

....

....

....

18. Do you think your local *community* regard you as a 'proper priest'?

Yes ☐

No ☐

If your answer is "yes", please move to question 20.

19. Please give an example to illustrate how the local community does not regard you as a 'proper priest'.

....

....

....

20. Do you think your local *congregation* regard you as a 'proper priest'?

Yes ☐

No ☐

If your answer is "yes", please move to question 22.

21. Please give an example to illustrate how the local congregation does not regard you as a 'proper priest'.

....

....

....

22. Do you think the *other clergy in your benefice* regard you as a 'proper priest'?

Yes ☐

No ☐

No other clergy in benefice ☐

If your answer is 'yes', please move to question 24

23. Please give an example to illustrate how the other clergy in your benefice do not regard you as a full member of the priesthood.

....

....

....

24. Do you think the *other clergy in your Chapter* regard you as a 'proper priest'?

Yes ☐

No ☐

If your answer is 'yes', please move to question 26.

25. Please give an example to illustrate how the other clergy in your Chapter do not regard you as a full member of the priesthood.

....

....

....

26. In an average month, how many times do you preach at a Sunday service in your benefice? ☐

27. In an average month, how many times do you celebrate the Eucharist on Sunday in your benefice? ☐

28. Last year, how many services did you take outside your benefice but within the deanery? ☐

29. Last year, how many services did you take outside the deanery but within the diocese? ☐

30. Last year, how many services did you take outside the diocese? ☐

31. Last year, how many people did you baptize? ☐

32. Last year, how many couples did you marry? ☐

33. Last year, how many people did you bury? □

34. In the course of your ministry, which *two* people/groups
    have been most helpful to you when you have needed support?

    Select no more than two.

Bishop	□
Archdeacon	□
Rural Dean	□
Incumbent	□
Other clergy	□
Family	□
Friends	□
Other (*please specify*)	□

    ....

35. Who is the *one* person you usually report to?
    Please select one.

The incumbent	□
NSM	□
Other (*please specify*)	□

    ....

36. Do you often find it difficult to attend meetings of the Deanery
    Chapter?

    Yes □

    No □

    If your answer is 'no', please move to question 38.

37. Why do you find it difficult to attend meetings of the deanery
    chapter?

    ....

    ....

38. Do you feel you have the same access to the bishop as stipendiary clergy?

    Yes ☐

    No ☐

39. If the bishop sends a letter to all clergy, does your copy come directly to you via a stipendiary?

    Direct ☐

    via stipendiary ☐

40. Has there been a change in incumbent since your ordination?

    Yes ☐

    If your answer is 'no', please move to question 44.   No ☐

41. Was your advice on the appointment of the new incumbent sought?

    Yes ☐

    No ☐

42. Do you feel the new incumbent is comfortable with the principle of local non-stipendiary ministry?

    Yes ☐

    No ☐

    If your answer if 'yes', please move to question 44.

43. Please give an example to illustrate why you feel the new incumbent is not comfortable with the principle of local non-stipendiary ministry.

    ....

    ....

    ....

APPRAISAL AND TRAINING

44. Has your Team and/or parish ever been appraised?

    If your answer is 'no', please move to question 48. Yes ☐

    No ☐

45. Who carried out the appraisal? Rural Dean ☐

    Other (*please specify*) ☐

    ....

46. Which year was the appraisal carried out? ☐

47. How did the appraisal help the Team/parish to develop?

    ....

    ....

48. Has your own ministry ever been appraised? Yes ☐

    If your answer is 'no', please move to question 52. No ☐

49. Who carried out your appraisal? Incumbent ☐

    Rural Dean ☐

    Other (please specify) ☐

    ....

50. Which year was the appraisal carried out? ☐

51. How did your appraisal help you to develop your ministry?

    ....

    ....

52. Would you like your own ministry to be appraised within the next year?

    Yes ☐

    No ☐

    Do not know ☐

53. What In-Service Training (CME) have you received?

    Please tick all that apply. Study day ☐

    Residential course ☐

    Regular course of several sessions ☐

    Other (please specify) ☐

    ....

54. What In-Service Training (CME) did you take part in during 1995?

    Please tick all that apply. Study day ☐

    Residential course ☐

    Regular course of several sessions ☐

    Other (please specify) ☐

    ....

55. Since January 1995, have you attended these events?

    Please tick all that apply. Annual Retreat ☐

    Christian Assembly ☐

    (e.g. Spring Harvest)

56. Do you have a spiritual director and/or soul friend? Yes ☐

    No ☐

ORDINATION

57. Which *two* people/groups gave you the initial encouragement to consider ordination?

    Please tick one box to indicate the most important person/group

    Incumbent ☐

    Other priest ☐

    Other member of ☐

    Local Ministry Team ☐

    Family ☐

    Friends ☐

    Other (please specify) ☐

    ....

58. In what ways has your personal life changed since ordination?

Please tick one of the boxes on each row to show the degree to which your life has changed.

My family life is more satisfying.	☐	☐	☐	☐	☐	My family life is less satisfying.
I feel my relationships with friends have become uncomfortable.	☐	☐	☐	☐	☐	I feel my relationships with friends have become closer.
Friends' expectations of me are no higher than before.	☐	☐	☐	☐	☐	Friends now have higher expectations of me.
Relationships with other members of the Local Ministry Team have declined.	☐	☐	☐	☐	☐	Relationships with other members of the Local Ministry Team have improved.
People at work now have higher expectations of me than before.	☐	☐	☐	☐	☐	People at work do not have higher expectations of me than before.
I have a better social life.	☐	☐	☐	☐	☐	I feel more socially isolated.
My health has declined as a result of my new role.	☐	☐	☐	☐	☐	My health has improved as a result of my new role.
Generally, I feel happier in myself.	☐	☐	☐	☐	☐	Generally, I feel less happy in myself.
I have had to make sacrifices in my personal life as a result of my new role.	☐	☐	☐	☐	☐	I have not had to make sacrifices in my personal life as a result of my new role.
I deeply regret having been ordained.	☐	☐	☐	☐	☐	Being ordained has given me great joy.

59. What effect has ordination had on your family?

....

....

....

60. If you wish to say anything more about the ways in which your personal life has changed since ordination, please use the space below.

....

....

....

ABOUT YOU

61. We realize that it may be difficult to classify your views and position in the Church. However, please could you tick *one* of these boxes?

Conservative Evangelical ☐

Open Evangelical ☐

Central ☐

Modern Catholic ☐

Traditional Catholic ☐

62. Please tick any of these boxes if they also apply to you.

Charismatic/renewal ☐

Liberal ☐

Radical ☐

63. What is your sex?

Female ☐

Male ☐

64. Which of these family members are members of your household at present?

    Please tick those that apply, and write the number in each category in the larger boxes.

    Spouse/partner ☐

    Children under 18 ☐
    How many?

    Children 18 and over ☐
    How many?

    Other(s) ☐
    How many?

65. At what age did you leave full-time education?　16 or under ☐
    17-19 ☐
    20-25 ☐
    Over 25 ☐

66. Which of these qualifications do you have?

    Please tick all that apply.　O Level(s)/CSEs/GCSEs ☐
    A Level(s) ☐
    Degree ☐
    Higher Degree(s) ☐
    Vocational or Professional Qualification(s) ☐
    (please specify)

    ....

    ....

67. If any of your qualifications are in Religious Education or a similar subject, please give details here.

    ....

    ....

68. What was your employment status at the time of your ordination?

    In full-time paid employment ☐

In part-time paid employment ☐
Unemployed and looking for work ☐
Homemaker ☐
Retired ☐

69. What was your job at the time of your ordination (or, if you were not in paid employment, the last job for which you had paid employment)?

Please give job title and a brief description of the main responsibilities.

....

....

70. What is your employment status now?

In full-time paid employment ☐
In part-time paid employment ☐
Unemployed and looking for work ☐
(please move to question 72)

Homemaker ☐
(please move to question 72)

Retired ☐
(please move to question 72)

71. What is your job now?
Please give job title and a brief description of the main responsibilities.

....

72. Do you have access to a car which is available for you to drive on a daily basis?

Yes ☐
No ☐

73. What are your current hobbies or other activities outside of your work and your ministry?

....

....

74. Before you were ordained, did you have any particular role within the church (in this benefice or elsewhere)? *Please specify.*

....

....

75. In which year were you born?

76. Do you live in the benefice in which you have your ministry?

If your answer is 'no', please move to question 79.   Yes ☐

No ☐

77. How long have you lived in this benefice?

Fewer than five years ☐

Five to ten years ☐

More than ten years ☐

78. Immediately before you lived in this benefice, where did you live?

Please move to question 80.   Always lived here ☐

Lived elsewhere in the diocese ☐

Lived outside the diocese ☐

79. If you do not live in the benefice in which you have your ministry, please give details (e.g. just over the boundary, in temporary accommodation etc.).

....

80. What kind of housing do you live in?   Privately rented ☐

Rented from Council ☐

Owner-occupied (with or without mortgage) ☐

81. Is there anything else you would like to say? Please use a separate sheet or overleaf.

THANK YOU FOR COMPLETING THE QUESTIONNAIRE NOW PLEASE MAIL IT BACK IN THE PRE-PAID ENVELOPE

APPENDIX 4

Ministry Development
and Deployment Committee

Working Group on the procedures
for recognition of LNSM Schemes

CRITERIA AND QUESTIONS

Name of LNSM scheme ....

1. How is the local parochial context and incumbent of the parish appraised and prepared for local non-stipendiary ministry? What is the relationship of the candidate to the parish during the initial training period?

2. (a) What is the procedure for drawing up a job description for the ordained person?

    (b) What is the length of term of the licence?

    (c) What are the procedures for ministerial review (appraisal of ministry)?

(d) How is the parish's participation in the diocesan LNSM scheme to be appraised and what are the procedures for extending or concluding it?

(e) Is there a procedure for incorporating new candidates from a parish that has already been in the LNSM scheme for some years?

(f) What is the provision for continuing ministerial education?

3. What are the procedures for review and evaluation of their diocesan LNSM scheme and what are the procedures for extending or concluding it?

4. When does ordination take place?

5.   What provision is made for oversight of a parish LNSM scheme during a parish vacancy?

6.   Does the diocesan scheme require that parish profiles prepared for vacancies in the parish would include a clear reference to participation of the parish in the LNSM scheme?

7.   How is the scheme managed and what is the role of the LNSM Officer?

8.   Are there any other features of the scheme which should be drawn to the attention of the Working Group?

Appendix 5

Transformative education

David Leslie

What is it ?

Transformative education describes a process of adult learning based on an interpretation of a person's life experience. It sometimes goes by other names, e.g. experiential learning, active learning.

Where does it come from ?

Transformative education is contextual and grows out of the philosophical, educational and psychological ideas which we use to interpret what we experience.

Models for transformative education – oscillation, circles and spirals

I find it helpful to describe the relation between the self and sense experience as a process of oscillation. Gadamer's great book *Truth and Method* (1960) describes the process as play – a 'to-and-fro movement that is not tied to any goal that would bring it to an end'.[1] The process may be conceived as a circle using the models of Lewin and Piaget in which reflection on experience leads to active experimentation.

This model, or something much like it, is frequently used by liberation theologians. It is described as 'the hermeneutic circle'.[2] We can think of it three-dimensionally because knowledge gained by travelling the full circle brings us to a new starting point.

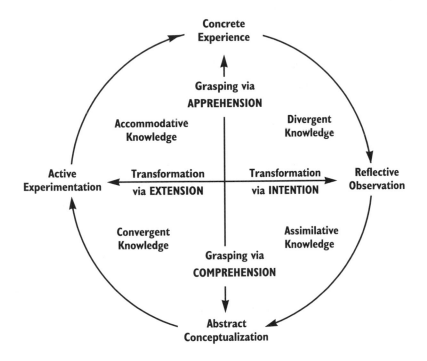

Figure 4: Structural dimensions underlying the process of experiental learning and the resulting basic knowledge forms, from David A. Kolb, *Experiential Learning: Experience as the Source of Learning and Development* (p. 42), © 1984. Reprinted by permission of Prentice-Hall, Inc., Upper Saddle River, NJ (see note 5).

These models provide us with pictures of how learning takes place.

Educational and psychological background

The educational philosophy of transformative education draws on the work of Dewey and Lewin. Dewey tried to throw some light on the conflict between his 'progressive' approach to education and 'traditional' education.[3] Lewin worked on group dynamics and the methodology of 'action research' which led to the setting up of training groups which proved to be a very significant educational innovation.[4]

Developmental psychology has also made a very important contribution to transformative education. Jean Piaget showed how intelligence is shaped by experience in identifiable stages. Donald Winnicott and others have worked on 'object relations theory' which describes how a growing child relates to objective reality. Erik Erikson's 'Eight stages of Man' used Freud's ideas of 'conflict resolution' to map sequential stages of development which continue through the life-span. Lawrence Kohlberg used conflict resolution to describe a person's moral development by posing a number of ethical dilemmas.[5]

Faith development theory

James Fowler and Fritz Oser[6] have combined the findings of the educationalists and developmental psychologists to describe sequential 'stages of faith' which show how religious faith grows and changes through the life-span.

Transitions and trigger events

The developmental psychologists draw attention to the transitional interval between one stage and the next and to 'trigger events' which may occur at any moment in our lives.[7] It is these moments which provide the greatest potential for learning. Using the Jungian concept of 'differentiation/reintegration' – the yearning for independence and the yearning for inclusion – we may decide to resist moving on to the next stage or risk letting go. Perhaps the most painful of these transitions occurs when we need to move from a private religious faith enclosed within a nurturing environment to embrace ambiguity and paradox in the public and social sphere.

Educating for change

Transformative education is education for change. Developmental psychology helps us to see how learning takes place in a challenging environment. Paulo Freire, in a Latin American context, criticizes the 'banking system' of education where learners are seen as ' "containers" . . . receptacles to be filled by the teacher'.[8] He says that education consists of 'acts of cognition, not transferrals of information'.[9] Matias Preiswerk, also in Latin America, compares three contrasting methods for Christian education – 'spiritualistic' which is submissive, individualistic and predetermined; 'liberal', where education remains elitist, privatized and compartmentalized; 'liberative' where teacher and learners work together and relate what they learn to the world as they experience it.[10]

Thinking critically

Helping adults to think critically is a fundamentally important part of transformative education. It is to be aware of our 'ideological immersion' (Freire). Thinking critically, 'seeing through things', applies in every context, not just in Latin America. It enables us to become aware of our local and personal ideological enclosures. Transformative education, therefore, also draws on the insights of the western critical theorists.[11] Thinking critically enables teachers and learners to be more sharply aware of their particular learning context and the constraints put on it.[12]

From private and competitive to public and collaborative

Learning with others helps each individual learner to gain from the insights of other members of the group. It provides a testing environment which assists the painful transition from a private and competitive understanding of learning to one which welcomes collaboration with others in a public and social setting.

Teachers and learners

Teachers need to be sensitive to what the learners know already and make sure that new theory and information is understood before moving on. They need to encourage learners to look critically at their experience. They need to allow time for working in groups and for reporting back.

Assessment

Assessment may take the form of a written exercise but is more likely to take the form of an oral presentation or group discussion which pulls together the theme, the experience of the learners and the purpose of the course in the light of agreed learning outcomes. Keeping a learning journal plays a very important part in making an overall assessment of the learning process for each individual learner.

Why transformative education?

We have seen that a transformative educational method enables adults to apply their experience of life to a chosen area of study. It enables learners to think critically and avoid the compartmentalization of knowledge. It encourages learners to connect what they learn with their local context. It assists learners in their personal development as they negotiate periods of transition in their lives, particularly the transition from a private and elitist understanding of education to one which recognizes its public and social implications. Transformative education is both personally and socially transformative.[13]

Transformative education and LNSM

Transformative education is being increasingly used in adult education.[14] While its relevance to the training of all who exercise ministry in the Church should not be underestimated, it would seem to be particularly appropriate for men and women training to be LNSMs in the Church of England.

Notes to Appendix 5

1. Hans Georg Gadamer, *Truth and Method*, (1960), Sheed and Ward, London, 1975

2. See, for example, J. L. Segundo, *The Liberation of Theology*, Orbis Books, Maryknoll, N.Y., 1976, pp. 7–38.

3. J. Dewey, *Experience and Education*, Kappa Delta Pi, 1938.

4. K. Lewin, *Field Theory in Social Sciences,* Harper and Row, New York, 1951.

5. Much of this paragraph is well documented in David A. Kolb, *Experiential Learning: Experience as the Source of Learning and Development*, Prentice-Hall, Inc., Englewood Cliffs, New Jersey, 1984.

6. J. Fowler, *Stages of Faith*, Harper and Row, San Francisco,1981; F. Oser and P. Gmunder, *Religious Judgement*, Religious Education Press, Birmingham, Alabama, 1991.

7. The educationalists Stephen Brookfield and Patricia Cranton make much of 'trigger events'. See S. Brookfield, *Developing Critical Thinkers*, Open University Press, Milton Keynes, 1987; P. Cranton, *Transformative Learning*, Jossey Bass, San Francisco, 1994.

   For 'transitions', Robert Kegan's book draws on the work of Piaget and Kohlberg. See R. Kegan, *The Evolving Self*, Harvard University Press, Cambridge, Massachusetts, 1982.

   For 'transitions' and religious faith see the faith development literature and J.M.Hull, *What Prevents Christian Adults From Learning?*, (1985), Trinity Press International, Philadelphia, 1991.

8. P. Freire, *Pedagogy of the Oppressed*, Penguin, 1972, p. 45.

9. *Ibid.* p. 53.

10. M. Preiswerk, *Educating in the Living Word*, Orbis Books, Maryknoll, New York, 1987.

11. The Frankfurt School of Philosophy, Adorno, Horkheimer and others.

12. See note 7 above. Cranton's book provides a good summary of transformative education.

13. See *Educating for a Change*, a handbook produced by Between the Lines and

the Doris Marshall Institute for Education and Action, Toronto, 1991.

See also for example modules eleven and twelve of a twelve-module pack produced by the Universities' Staff Development Unit, B. Brown and M. Pendelbury, *Module 11: Effective Learning and Teaching in Higher Education*, CVCP Universities' Staff Development and Training Unit, Sheffield, 1992; M. O'Neil and G. Pennington, *Module 12: Evaluating Teaching and Courses from an Active Learning Perspective*, CVCP Universities' Staff Development and Training Unit, Sheffield, 1992.

Bibliography

ACORA, *Faith in the Countryside*, Arthur Rank Centre, NAC, Stoneleigh Park, Warks, Acora Publishing, 1990.

ACUPA, *Faith in the City*, London: Church House Publishing, 1989.

Advisory Board of Ministry, Ministry Paper No. 16, *The Care of Candidates*, London, 1997.

Advisory Board of Ministry, Policy Paper No. 1, *Local NSM*, London: Church House Publishing, 1991.

Advisory Board of Ministry, Policy Paper No. 3A, *Criteria for Selection for Ministry in the Church of England*, London: Church House Publishing, 1993.

Advisory Board of Ministry, Policy Paper No. 4, *Development of Models of Ministry and Training in Recent Diocesan Proposals for LNSM,* London: Church House Publishing, 1992.

Advisory Board of Ministry, Policy Paper No. 5, *Order in Diversity*, London: Church House Publishing, 1993.

Advisory Board of Ministry, Policy Paper No. 6, *A Review of Selection Procedures in the Church of England*, London: Church House Publishing, 1995.

Advisory Board of Ministry, Policy Paper No. 15, *Issues in Theological Education and Training*, London: Church House Publishing, 1997.

Allen Roland *see* Paton, D.M.

Baker, J., *Salisbury Diocese: Ministerial Resource and Deployment,* Green Paper. Salisbury: Diocesan Office, 1992.

Beaminster Parish, *Team Handbook*, Beaminster: Parish Office, 1982.

Bishops' Conference of England and Wales, *The Sign We Give — Report from the Working Party on Collaborative Ministry*, Chelmsford: Matthew, James Publishing, 1995.

Blythe, R., *Akenfield*, London: Allen Lane, The Penguin Press, 1969.

Blythe, R., *Divine Landscapes*, London: Viking, 1986.

Board of Mission of the General Synod of the Church of England, Occasional Paper No. 6, *A Time for Sharing*, London: Church House Publishing, 1995.

Board of Education of the General Synod of the Church of England, *All Are Called. Towards a Theology of the Laity*, London: CIO, 1985.

Boff, L., *Ecclesiogenesis: The Base Communities Reinvent the Church*, Maryknoll, New York: Orbis Books, 1986.

Bracegirdle, C., *Changing Patterns of Ministry in the Diocese of Manchester — The Impact of LNSM*, unpublished paper submitted for Clergy Course at St George's House, Windsor, 1996.

Bradbury, N., 'The minister as midwife', *Theology*, Vol. XCVI, No. 774, November 1993, pp. 444–7.

Clark, P., Goodwin, M. and Milbourne, P., *Rural Wales: Community and Marginalisation*, Cardiff: University of Wales Press, 1997.

Cloke, P. and Edwards, G., 'Rurality in England and Wales 1981: a replication of the 1971 index', *Regional Studies*, 1986, No. 20, pp. 289–306.

Cloke, P., Goodwin, M. and Milbourne, P., *Lifestyles in Rural Wales. Report to the Development Board for Rural Wales,* Newtown, 1994.

Cloke, P. and Milbourne, P., 'Deprivation and lifestyles in rural Wales. Rurality and the cultural dimension', *Journal of Rural Studies*, 1992, Vol.8, No. 4, pp. 359–71.

Cohen, R., *Frontiers of Identity: The British and the Others*. London: Macmillan, 1994.

Cope, S., 'The role of the laity in the rural Church', BTh thesis, University of Southampton, 1987.

Coventry, Diocese of, *Guidelines for the Ministry*, Coventry: Diocesan Office, 1991.

Davie, R., *Religion in Britain since 1945*, Oxford: Blackwell, 1994.

Davies, D. J., Watkins, C. and Winter, M., *Church and Religion in Rural England*, Edinburgh: T. & T. Clark, 1991.

Diocesan Submissions to ABM for LNSM schemes; various held at Church House, Westminster.

Donaldson, C., *The New Springtime of the Church*, Norwich: Canterbury Press, 1992.

Ecclestone, G. (ed.), *The Parish Church?*, London: Mowbray, 1988.

Ely, Diocese of, *Ministry: A Report to the Bishop from the Ministry Advisory Group*. Ely: Diocesan Office, 1988.

Evreux, Diocese of , *La Pastorale Rurale d'accompagnement (Eglise en marche,* No. 12). Evreux: Diocese d'Evreux, 1990.

Francis, L.J., *Rural Anglicanism*, London: Collins, 1985.

Francis, L. J., 'The rural rectory: the impact of a resident priest on local church life', *Journal of Rural Studies*, 1992, Vol. 8, No.1, pp. 97–103.

General Synod, *Deployment of the Clergy* (The Sheffield Report), Report of the House of Bishops' Working Group, London: GS 205, 1974.

General Synod of the Church of England, *Team and Group Ministries: Report of the Working Party* (GS 993), London: 1991.

General Synod of the Church of England, *Team and Group Ministries Measure* (GS 994), London: 1992.

General Synod of the Church of England, *Team and Group Ministries: A Report by the Ministry Co-ordinating Group* (GS 660), London: 1985.

Gill, R., *Beyond Decline*, London: SCM Press, 1992.

Gill, R., *The Myth of the Empty Church*, London: SPCK, 1993.

Graham, A., *Priesthood Here and Now*, one of a series of leaflets on priesthood produced by ABM, London: Church House Publishing, 1995.

Greenwood, R., *Transforming Priesthood*, London: SPCK, 1994.

Greenwood, R., *Practising Community*, London: SPCK, 1996.

Halsey, A. H., *Change in British Society 1900 to the Present Day*, Oxford: Opus, 4th edition, 1995.

Hammersley, J., *Working Together in Teams and Groups*, Parish and People, The Old Mill, Spetisbury, Blandford Forum, Dorset, 1989.

Ineson, H., *LNSM Training — What are we Doing?*, unpublished paper, 1995.

Kent Agricultural Chaplaincy, Local Ordained Ministry, Pluckley: Revd J. Sage, 1980.

Legg, R., *Lay Pastorate*, East Wittering: Angel Press, 1989.

Leominster Team Ministry, *Annual Report*, Leominster: The Rectory, 1992.

Lewis, C., 'The practice of the absence of the priest', *New Fire*, Winter 1982.

Lewis, R. and Talbot-Ponsonby, A., *The People, the Land and the Church*, Hereford: Hereford Diocesan Board of Finance, 1987.

Lincoln, Diocese of, *Exploring Local Ministry*, Lincoln: Diocesan Office, 1990.

Lincoln, Diocese of, *Five Course Books in Local Ministry*, Lincoln: Diocesan Office, 1990.

Lincoln, Diocese of, Local Ministry Scheme. Submission to ABM, Lincoln: Diocesan Office, 1990.

Lincoln, Diocese of, *New Times, New Ways — Report by Bishop to Synod*, Lincoln: Diocesan Office, 1991.

Lincoln, Diocese of, St Hugh Missioner, *Using the Vacancy Constructively,* Lincoln: Diocesan Office, no date.

Lossky, V., *The Mystical Theology of the Eastern Church,* London: James Clarke, 1957.

Macquarrie, J., *The Faith of the People of God,* London: SCM Press, 1972.

Marr, A., *Ruling Britannia,* London: Penguin, 1995.

Mason, K., *Priesthood and Society,* Norwich: Canterbury Press, 1992.

Mathieson, M., *Delectable Mountains: The Story of the Washington County Mission Program,* Cincinnati: Forward Movement Publications, 1979.

Mayne, M., *The Sunrise of Wonder,* London: Fount, 1995.

Neale, G., Lincoln *Local Ministry Scheme: the Praxis,* MA dissertation presented to University of Hull, 1995.

Nott, P., *Moving Forward,* Norwich: Diocesan House, 1989.

Nott, P., *Moving Forward II,* Norwich: Diocesan House, 1991.

Paton, D. M. (ed.), *Reform of the Ministry: A Study of the Work of Roland Allen,* London: Lutterworth, 1968.

Paul, L., *The Deployment and Payment of the Clergy* (Paul Report), London: CIO, 1964.

Rahner, K., *The Shape of the Church to Come,* London: SPCK, 1974.

Ripon, Diocese of, *Two Years on – Local Ministry in 1985,* Ripon: Diocesan House, 1985.

Ripon, Diocese of, *Review of the Local Ministry Scheme,* Ripon: Diocesan House, 1989.

Roberts, E., *Partners and Minister,* London: Falcon Books, 1972.

Royle, S., *A Theological Basis for LNSM,* Salisbury: Canon S. Royle, 1992.

Russell, A. (ed.), *Groups and Teams in the Countryside,* London: SPCK, 1975.

Russell, A., *The Clerical Profession,* London: SPCK, 1980.

Russell, A., *The Country Parish,* London: SPCK, 1986.

Russell, A., *The Country Parson,* London: SPCK, 1993.

Rutter, C., *Local Ordained Ministry,* Salisbury: Diocesan Office, 1989.

Salisbury, Diocese of, *Going with God – Together,* Salisbury: Diocesan Office, 1990.

Salisbury, Diocese of, *Ministerial Resources and Deployment, A Green Paper on Long Term Planning,* Salisbury: Diocesan Office, 1992.

Smethurst, D., *Extended Communion: An Experiment in Cumbria*, Nottingham: Grove Books, 1986.

Smith, A. C., *The South Ormsby Experiment: An Adventure in Friendship*, London: SPCK, 1960.

Stewart, J., *Parson to Parson*, Langton Matravers: The Rectory, 1988.

Tiller, J., *A Strategy for the Church's Ministry* (Tiller Report), London: CIO, 1983.

Tiller, J. and Birchall, M., *The Gospel Community and Its Leadership*, Basingstoke: Marshall Pickering, 1987.

Truro, Diocese of, *Local Non-Stipendiary Ministry in the Diocese of Truro: Report by Bishop of Truro's Working Party*, Truro: Diocesan Office, 1992.

Turner, H. J.M., (1987) 'Ordination and vocation', *Sobornost*, Vol. 9, No 1. London: Fellowship of St Alban and St Sergius, 1987.

Van de Weyer, R., *The Country Church*, London: Darton, Longman & Todd, 1991.

West, M., *Second Class Priests with Second Class Training? – A Study of L.N.S.M.* PhD thesis submitted to the University of East Anglia, 1994.

White, G., *The Natural History and Antiquities of Selbourne*, numerous editions, 1789.

Williams, W.M., *The Sociology of an English Village: Gosforth*, London: Routledge, 1956.

Winchester, Diocese of, *Lay Pastor's Training Course*, Winchester: Diocesan Office, 1984.

Winchester, Diocese of, *A Church for the World*. Report of the Ordained Ministry Review Group, Winchester: Diocesan Office, 1990.

Many Anglican Dioceses in USA, Canada, Australia and New Zealand are experimenting with 'Local Ministry' in one form or another. Of particular interest are Northern Michigan USA, Perth, Australia and Christchurch, New Zealand.